PUCCINI'S *LA BOHÈME*

Oxford KEYNOTES
Series Editor   KEVIN BARTIG

PUCCINI'S
LA BOHÈME

ALEXANDRA WILSON

OXFORD
UNIVERSITY PRESS

Oxford University Press is a department of the University of Oxford. It furthers
the University's objective of excellence in research, scholarship, and education
by publishing worldwide. Oxford is a registered trade mark of Oxford University
Press in the UK and certain other countries.

Published in the United States of America by Oxford University Press
198 Madison Avenue, New York, NY 10016, United States of America.

Library of Congress Cataloging-in-Publication Data
Names: Wilson, Alexandra, 1973– author.
Title: Puccini's La bohème / Alexandra Wilson.
Description: New York : Oxford University Press, 2021. |
Includes bibliographical references and index.
Identifiers: LCCN 2020018916 (print) | LCCN 2020018917 (ebook) |
ISBN 9780190637880 (hardback) | ISBN 9780190637897 (paperback) |
ISBN 9780190637910 (epub) | ISBN 9780190637903 (updf) | ISBN 9780190637927 (online)
Subjects: LCSH: Puccini, Giacomo, 1858–1924. Bohème.
Classification: LCC ML410.P89 W532 2020 (print) |
LCC ML410.P89 (ebook) | DDC 782.1—dc23
LC record available at https://lccn.loc.gov/2020018916
LC ebook record available at https://lccn.loc.gov/2020018917

9 8 7 6 5 4 3 2 1
Paperback printed by LSC Communications, United States of America
Hardback printed by Bridgeport National Bindery, Inc., United States of America

Series Editor's
INTRODUCTION

O XFORD KEYNOTES REIMAGINES THE canons of Western music for the twenty-first century. With each of its volumes dedicated to a single composition or album, the series provides an informed, critical, and provocative companion to music as artwork and experience. Books in the series explore how works of music have engaged listeners, performers, artists, and others through history and in the present. They illuminate the roles of musicians and musics in shaping Western cultures and societies, and they seek to spark discussion of ongoing transitions in contemporary musical landscapes. Each approaches its key work in a unique way, tailored to the distinct opportunities that the work presents. Targeted at performers, curious listeners, and advanced undergraduates, volumes in the series are written by expert and engaging voices in their fields, and will therefore be of significant interest to scholars and critics as well.

In selecting titles for the series, Oxford Keynotes balances two ways of defining the canons of Western music: as lists of works that critics and scholars deem to have articulated key moments in the history of the art, and as lists of works that comprise the bulk of what consumers listen to, purchase, and perform today. Often, the two lists intersect, but the overlap is imperfect. While not neglecting the first, Oxford Keynotes gives considerable weight to the second. It confronts the musicological canon with the living repertoire of performance and recording in classical, popular, jazz, and other idioms. And it seeks to expand that living repertoire through the latest musicological research.

Kevin Bartig
Michigan State University

COVER IMAGE.
Costume for the character of Mimì for the opera *La bohème* by Giacomo Puccini. Watercolour by Adolfo Hohenstein. Photograph © Giancarlo Costa / Bridgeman Images.

Ho tante cose che ti voglio dire, o una sola, ma grande come il mare, come il mare profonda ed infinita . . .

Mimì, Act 4, *La bohème*

CONTENTS

FIGURES

ACKNOWLEDGEMENTS

I AM INDEBTED TO THE many people who have contributed, directly or indirectly, to shaping my thoughts on *La bohème* and who supported me during the writing of this book. First and foremost, I must thank Kevin Karnes, Oxford Keynotes series editor, for inviting me to write the book and for his sage advice throughout the writing process. I am grateful to Suzanne Ryan, Commissioning Editor at Oxford University Press, for giving the project the green light. Enthusiastic and perceptive comments from anonymous readers at both the commissioning and peer review stages helped me to write a better book. Tim Lloyd and Mahima Macchione assisted me in tracking down French and South American reviews. Mark Berry shared valuable thoughts on different directorial interpretations of the opera. Dai Griffiths and Jan Butler offered their expertise on cover versions. Twitter followers too numerous to name individually directed me towards extracts from *La bohème* in popular culture. Hugo Shirley generously read an early draft of the manuscript. Hugh Canning kindly took me to see the new Royal Opera House production in 2017, giving me a chance to hear the wonderful Benjamin Bernheim as Rodolfo. David Crown lifted my spirits by teaching me to sing Mimì's aria.

I completed the manuscript and leapt through all the final administrative hoops to push it into production in the early spring of 2020. This was an incredibly testing moment at which to be attempting to finish a book, yet at the same time I welcomed the distraction that the challenge offered. I am supremely grateful to the people who helped me at what was a stressful time for everyone. Paul Parker read the final manuscript, helped me source pictures and secure permissions, and offered characteristically cheerful encouragement as I approached the finishing line. Michael Volpe showed kindness I shall never forget. Sian Phillips at Bridgeman Images helped me to obtain the cover image in difficult circumstances. Over in New York, Norm Hirschy at Oxford University Press was unfailingly patient, helpful, and quick to respond to last-minute queries. At home, Andrew Timms heroically took over the domestic reins almost entirely; little Sebastian worked hard so that I could work hard too and helped me to smile. My sincerest thanks to them all.

Alexandra Wilson
Abingdon, March 2020

SETTING THE SCENE

I T IS, ON THE face of it, the simplest of dramatic premises: boy meets girl, boy and girl separate, girl dies. And yet from this slim material, Puccini and his librettists succeeded in creating an opera that, over a period of more than 120 years, has withstood repeated—extremely repeated—listening. *La bohème* is surely among the most romantic of romantic operas, with its exquisite evocation of a serendipitous encounter, the moment at which a spark of passion ignites, summed up—with no great subtlety but maximum effectiveness—by the re-illuminated flame of Mimì's candle. This is, furthermore, an opera that confronts in frank and unflinching fashion a set of inescapable truths about the passing of time: the fleetingness of youth, the inexorable ticking of the clock, the importance of seizing the

Puccini's La bohème. Alexandra Wilson, Oxford University Press (2021). © Oxford University Press.
DOI: 10.1093/oso/9780190637880.001.0001.

moment. My personal love affair with *La bohème* is doubtless already apparent, and yet there is of course more to this opera than the way in which it presses our emotional buttons—gratifyingly or manipulatively, depending on your point of view. It is a work that tapped at the time of its creation into a set of contemporary cultural tropes—about Paris, about art, about poverty—and that has given them enduring life across a prolonged period both within and beyond the opera house. This last point is key: of all operas, *La bohème* has surely had one of the most significant impacts as a cultural artefact beyond the parameters of its own artistic genre.

What more could there possibly be to say, then, about this exceptionally well-known work? Matters of genesis, libretto, musical style, and compositional process have already been comprehensively analysed in other books.[1] I do not therefore address these topics in substance here, although I revisit them briefly in the opening chapter for the benefit of the reader who is encountering the opera for the first time or not acquainted with the specialist Puccini literature. But this book is in essence a cultural history of *La bohème*, which places the opera within the artistic and social contexts of its day. Opera in turn-of-the-century Italy wasn't simply entertainment: as an art form intimately connected with the national self-image, it had vital political work to do.

The book also investigates how *La bohème*'s musical, dramatic, and socio-cultural significance has evolved since its première in 1896. In the present-day canon of popular operas, *La bohème* surely sits at the apex, together with works such as *La traviata* and *Carmen*: the opera will rarely be absent from the repertory of any major opera company for more than a few seasons. (Herbert Lindenberger expresses the point rather less forgivingly, featuring *La bohème* in a list of operatic 'warhorses': works that 'can fill the house even if the cast has to be pulled off the street and the backdrops and costumes reveal their moth holes well into the orchestra section'.[2]) Although the opera's accession to this position was comparatively swift, it was by no means initially guaranteed. One turn-of-the-century American critic summed up the tenor of a good number of the early reviews with the words '*La bohème* is not a great work. It is not even a good one, and it will not live long'.[3] Furthermore, the opera was not immune to controversy during Puccini's lifetime. Despite its colossal popularity—or perhaps indeed precisely because of that popularity—*La bohème* cannot be separated from what I have referred to elsewhere as 'the Puccini Problem': a sense of anxiety about the interactions between high art and popular entertainment; concerns about how operatic works could or should articulate the pressing political and social issues of the day; and fears for the future of the operatic art form itself.[4]

Although certain aspects of *La bohème*'s rise to popularity are concrete and can be discussed systematically—the roles of certain recordings, performers, or stagings, for example—others are less tangible. The sheer emotional appeal of Puccini's music and approach to drama is one of the most important factors in assessing the work's success and yet it is difficult to pin down. Scholars have, for the most part, shied away from trying to grapple with how artworks make us feel, as if the very existence of an emotional response, let alone any sort of visceral one, would undermine an opera's, a novel's, or a play's credibility as an object of discussion. But one surely cannot avoid the subject in the case of a work such as *La bohème*. Of course, I do not ignore the fact that the opera does not captivate everyone: for every listener who melts at Rodolfo and Mimì's mutual seduction there is a Puccini-sceptic who baulks at what they see as calculating sentimentality. Both of these strands in the work's reception demand attention.

The first chapter of the book considers how *La bohème* operates musically and dramatically and how Puccini handles characterisation and the opera's central themes of love, death, and nostalgia. Chapter 2, meanwhile, focuses upon Paris, examining the opera's treatment of geographical place, realism, and urban poverty. In the remaining chapters I analyse *La bohème*'s international reception and how its popularity spread, not only via theatrical performance but through recordings and its transfer to the screen. Chapter 3 focuses upon the opera's immediate critical reception in Italy, before identifying themes that emerged from its subsequent transnational reception, some of them widely shared, some of them specific to particular locations. Chapter 4 traces *La bohème*'s longer twentieth-century reception, interweaving the opera's encounters with popular culture with the responses of a hostile intelligentsia, and grappling with the question of where the opera sits on the spectrum between what constitutes art and what constitutes 'mere' entertainment.

Ascension to the musical canon is rarely instantaneous: an artwork has to serve its time, pay its dues. As early as the 1930s it was already clear that *La bohème* had become, in the biographer Vincent Seligman's words, 'the opera on which Puccini's claim to immortality most securely rests.'[5] Yet around the same time, some commentators were already beginning to question whether the opera had passed its sell-by date. Indefinite canonical status can never be absolutely guaranteed for any artwork; indeed, over-familiarity, as in any other sphere of life, can sometimes breed contempt. So regularly performed is our work that opera companies now have to guard against the possibility of *Bohème* fatigue. Thus, the final chapter of the book examines the ways in which directors have, in the twenty-first century, sought to reinvent *La bohème* for a new age. Our journey will take us to grungy hipster apartments, to a clinical hospital ward, even to the moon. I hope it will be an exciting one, as we discover, or rediscover, this multi-layered work, in which there is something new to observe with every fresh encounter.

CHAPTER 1

LA BOHÈME *IN CONTEXT*

H E MIGHT SO EASILY have been a one-hit wonder. Puccini had established himself on the international operatic circuit in 1893 with his third opera, *Manon Lescaut*, but one triumph was no guarantee of another. Whereas the leading Italian opera composers of earlier generations had produced hit after hit in quick succession, the operatic environment of the turn of the twentieth century seemed harder to navigate. Despite all being highly productive across many decades, Puccini's contemporaries Pietro Mascagni, Ruggero Leoncavallo, and Umberto Giordano would fail to follow up on the success they had achieved with *Cavalleria rusticana* (1890), *Pagliacci* (1892), and *Andrea Chénier* (1896) respectively.

Puccini's La bohème. Alexandra Wilson, Oxford University Press (2021). © Oxford University Press.
DOI: 10.1093/oso/9780190637880.001.0001.

Across the course of his career, Puccini toyed with, and subsequently discarded, numerous literary subjects as the basis for operatic adaptations. But within weeks of the *Manon Lescaut* première, Puccini had seized upon Henry Murger's bohemian tales as a guaranteed crowd pleaser, and he remained resolute about his decision even when his publisher Giulio Ricordi tried to persuade him of the difficulties of adapting such material. This would be Puccini's first collaboration with the librettists Luigi Illica and Giuseppe Giacosa (see figure 1.1), both well-known writers outside of the operatic arena. The partnership proved highly fruitful—resulting in Puccini's so-called big three operas, *La bohème*, *Tosca*, and *Madama Butterfly*—and might have continued to be so had Giacosa not died in 1906. The three men developed a regular working pattern: Illica and Puccini would develop the initial dramatic concept of a work; Giacosa would versify the text; Puccini would compose the music in full; and Illica would step back into the picture at the post-compositional stage for any necessary dramatic revisions. Puccini himself would also take a hand in shaping the libretto, and Ricordi chipped in from time to time.

The working relationship was not always an easy one, however. In the case of *La bohème*, Giacosa and Illica struggled to keep Puccini focused as he promoted *Manon Lescaut* in various European cities, battled with self-doubt, and flirted with other potential operatic subjects. (Verga's *La lupa*, a story about a Sicilian *femme fatale*, was a notable distraction.) Composer and librettists argued back and forth by letter for almost two years about the ideal dramatic structure of *La bohème*, which led to Puccini making endless modifications to the draft score and constantly requesting

FIGURE 1.1   Giacomo Puccini (1858–1924), Italian composer, with Giuseppe
Giacosa (1847–1906), playwright, and Luigi Illica (1857–1919),
playwright and librettist / De Agostini Picture Library / A. Dagli
Orti / Bridgeman Images.

that sections of libretto be rewritten. The genesis of the
work was also complicated by a dispute between Puccini
and Leoncavallo, who was writing a *La bohème* of his own.
Puccini was reasonably nonchalant about the competition,

writing with a metaphorical shrug of the shoulders that the public would make the final judgement.[1] Nevertheless, the fact that the two men seized upon the same subject at the same time led to a highly public spat conducted largely in the pages of the press.

The French author Henry Murger's bohemian tales had first appeared as a series of short stories, serialised in a Parisian magazine, *Le Corsaire Satan*, during the second half of the 1840s. Murger subsequently collaborated with the dramatist Théodore Barrière to adapt the material as a play with songs (*La Vie de Bohème*, 1849) for the Parisian Théâtre des Variétés. Finally, Murger milked the material further by writing a novel, *Scènes de la vie de bohème* (1851), which is the direct, albeit rather loose, source for Puccini's opera. The novel would have been familiar to Italian readers from the 1872 translation entitled *La bohème: Scene della scapigliatura parigina*. The term 'Scapigliatura' (the 'dishevelled ones') was a topical one in the Italian context, referring specifically to a prominent group of painters, writers, and musicians who had been active in the artistic salons of Milan in the 1860s and 1870s.

Giacosa and Illica were faced with the daunting task of turning a rambling set of episodes into a coherent operatic narrative—something that prompted a negative reaction from some critics who remained wedded to a much-loved literary source. Any novel or play requires considerable compression in order to be turned into an opera libretto—words take longer to sing than to deliver in speech, and, in the case of most operas, prose needs to be turned into verse form—but in this instance the need was particularly acute.

The task at hand required omitting vast swathes of material, fleshing out small incidents, adjusting the novel's largely humorous tone, and amalgamating characters.

A reminder of the opera's plot reveals the conciseness of Giacosa and Illica's version of the story. In the first act we meet the poet Rodolfo and his lively Bohemian friends (the painter Marcello, the musician Schaunard, the philosopher Colline) in their Parisian garret around 1830. Rodolfo falls in love with the seamstress Mimì when she comes knocking at his door to ask for a light for her candle. Act 2 showcases the animated life of the Latin Quarter: Rodolfo and Mimì's sentimental relationship is contrasted with the more hot-headed off-and-on love affair between Marcello and the good-time girl Musetta. By Act 3 things have turned sour: Rodolfo and Mimì have separated, ostensibly because he is jealous of her flirtations, in truth because he cannot face up to her illness and their poverty. Act 4 mirrors Act 1 in taking us back to the jollity of the garret, although the bohemians' antics now have a bittersweet tint. Mimì arrives once more, this time not to fall in love but to die.

Illica initially regarded the plot as banal, writing to Ricordi: 'We have a meeting in an attic between a seamstress and a journalist. They love each other, they quarrel, then the seamstress dies. A sad story; but it is not *La bohème* . . . Mürger's Mimì is more complex'.[2] In the event, the sheer simplicity of Puccini, Giacosa, and Illica's interpretation of the *Bohème* story—which has long since surpassed Murger's as the defining version—gave it a universality that has undoubtedly contributed to the work's enduring popularity.

MUSICAL AND DRAMATIC CONTEXTS

La bohème's characters are humble, ordinary people, whatever their grandiose artistic pretensions, far removed from the operatic heroes and heroines of older eras. The way in which Rodolfo and Mimì introduce themselves to each other could scarcely be more prosaic: he tells us, with a shrug of the shoulders, that he simply 'lives' ('E come vivo? Vivo!'); she tells us a meandering story about her daily routine and—inconsequentially—the fact that her real name is Lucia. This is a realist opera but not, I would argue, a *verismo* one, and the reasons why are worth outlining.

Verismo is a term often used misleadingly for all Italian operas composed between the 1890s and the 1920s, but it more properly denotes a very specific style of opera written during that period, associated with the analogous Italian literary movement led by Giovanni Verga and Luigi Capuana. Mascagni's *Cavalleria rusticana* and Leoncavallo's *Pagliacci* are the most famous examples of operatic *verismo*. Such works were typically set in their composers' own era rather than in the past, in communities—whether urban or rural—suffering genuine deprivation. They tell sensationalist, low-life tales of lust, jealousy, and revenge (often involving a love triangle) and almost invariably culminate in gruesome crimes of passion. This is not the world in which we find ourselves in the altogether gentler *La bohème*. Musically, too, the typical hallmarks of *verismo*—shrieks, laughter, sobs, and a coarse style of musical writing that attempted to match the violence of the subject matter—are by and large absent here. *La bohème* is also compositionally more ambitious than the headline *verismo* operas, which often use a rather conservative pattern of arias and choruses, linked by simple recitative.

Nevertheless, Puccini was not averse to assimilating the musical trends of his era. Connections to the well-known mid-period works of Verdi are difficult to discern; however, the influence of *Falstaff* (1893), with its fast-paced musical language, is obvious. Meanwhile, no clued-up Italian composer of this period could escape the colossus that was Wagner, and Wagnerism would be a controversial theme in the reception of Puccini's music, as we shall see in due course. The German composer's influence is certainly apparent in *La bohème* in its lengthy through-composed passages, rich orchestral writing, use of motifs as a way of organising the score, and application, from time to time, of a chromatic harmonic palette, although Puccini employed these techniques in a very different way. *La bohème* is in essence something of a stylistic collage. Some commentators have criticised its composer for amalgamating a hotchpotch of stylistic influences and yet the final result could be by nobody other than Puccini: he has a sound that one reviewer described in 1897 as 'pronouncedly individual'.[3]

The opera's most distinguishing musical feature is the way in which Puccini cultivates a flexible, conversational style, which mimics the patterns of casual speech, and then contrasts this musical 'chatter' with moments of intensely memorable lyricism. He uses the first to convey topics of immense triviality, the second to convey the most heightened emotion. Wherever it might have sat in the contemporaneous musical landscape, there is little doubting the happy fit in *La bohème* between musical language and subject matter. As an American critic wrote in 1909, the music 'attempts to supply life-blood for the entire drama; to flow through its veins without ceasing; to bear along on its surface all the whims, emotions, follies, and incidents of the story as fast as they appear'.[4]

The music at the opera's opening is energetic and restless, the vocal parts not particularly lyrical except for moments of deliberate dramatic effect, the orchestra chipping in fitfully, constantly adapting itself to the twists and turns of the conversation rather than providing a constant accompaniment. This captures perfectly the youthful, carefree atmosphere of the students' rather chaotic lifestyle. Indeed, one of the most distinctive features of Puccini's musical realism—exhibited particularly well in *La bohème*—is the way in which he opens acts. His avoidance of a formal overture at the start of the opera (surely influenced by *Falstaff*) creates the impression that the music is already underway. This technique changes the relationship between us as audience members and the action onstage. We feel as though we have wandered in on the action part way through, taking on the role of eavesdroppers listening in on Rodolfo and Marcello as we peep through a window in the garret's roof. The same impression is created in Act 3, where the first two chords sound more like an ending than a beginning.

Dramatically, what Puccini offers us in this opera is a series of snapshots. Key scenes are not acted out in front of us: it is left up to us not only to imagine how Rodolfo seduces Mimì after their initial introduction but also to speculate to some extent about how their relationship has developed and foundered between Acts 2 and 3. Puccini is not interested so much in a continuously developing narrative—the big hallmark of the nineteenth-century novel—as he is in creating a set of sharply etched contrasts, alternating comic and sentimental or tragic episodes. Thus, the jolt we experience in moving rapidly from the intimate love scene in a private interior space at the end of Act 1 to the bustling, energetic street scene of Act 2 is entirely deliberate, and is felt both dramatically and musically (set-piece lyricism gives way to chaotic, fragmented street cries). The episodic nature of the opera was, of course, faithful to the literary source, which had been, as its title indicates, conceived as a series of 'scenes'.

As we shall see, many early critics were concerned by the opera's disjunctions, and it was a complaint that would resurface repeatedly. But the opera is by no means as haphazardly organised as it evidently seemed to those hearing it for the first time in 1896. There is a symmetry to the narrative arc of the work and Puccini is adroit in the way in which he draws together various dramatic threads through the use of recurring musical themes. We hear fragments of Mimì's Act 1 aria 'Sì, mi chiamano Mimì' as she tells Rodolfo in Act 3 that she must leave him and return to her old apartment. The heart-rending final act holds up a mirror to the more optimistic first: both take place in the same location, both begin with horseplay, both start with Rodolfo and Marcello alone together before their other friends turn up bearing food, both feature the arrival of Mimì. Both even commence with the same musical theme (somewhat truncated in the second instance), before we hear melodies associated with Musetta and Mimì as the two male leads reminisce about their former girlfriends. The seasons have ticked around and life goes on just as before, Puccini seems to suggest, at least until Mimì's second arrival, when the event that has been on the cards from the start can no longer be deferred. Here the memories come thick and fast, as the dying Mimì quotes directly from both her own introductory aria and from Rodolfo's.

LOVE AND FRIENDSHIP

Three key dramatic subjects that *La bohème* addresses are love, death, and nostalgia. The first two of these are ostensibly defining features of almost any nineteenth-century tragic opera, and yet—if we care to admit it—most operas deal with these subjects with barely a shred of genuine plausibility. Puccini's treatment of them, on the other hand, is sensitive and dramatically credible, and in this regard it was influenced by Verdi's *La traviata*, a landmark work of operatic realism. Both operas played into a fascination with the sufferings of the so-called *femme fragile*, a familiar archetype from mid nineteenth-century French literature. (Alexandre Dumas *fils'* *La Dame aux camélias*, the source for *La traviata*, was nearly contemporaneous with Murger's bohemian tales.) One American critic called Mimì 'Violetta Valery robbed of her good clothes, her jewels, and her champagne song.'[5]

In most nineteenth-century Italian operas of the tragic tradition, the romantic couple is thwarted by the intervention of a third party. This might be a father figure (*La traviata*), a jealous individual in a classic love triangle (*Pagliacci*), or some other malign force (*Otello*). Occasionally it is the hero himself—or more properly the anti-hero (the Duke of Mantua in *Rigoletto*)—who either by accident or by design brings about the heroine's demise. Across the course of his career, Puccini would draw upon some of these well-worn narrative archetypes. In particular, he deployed the love-triangle trope in those works in which he strayed closest to a *verismo* aesthetic: the hyper-theatrical *Tosca*, whose baritone is a sadistic torturer and would-be rapist, and the gritty, social realist *Il tabarro*, whose jealous baritone is treated somewhat more sympathetically. Meanwhile, the toxic tenor looms large in *Madama Butterfly*, even if the heroine ultimately dies at her own hand.

Interestingly, the opportunity to repeat the classic formula of the interfering older relative messing things up was there with *La bohème*: Murger's Rodolphe has a rich uncle who tries to persuade his nephew to give up his lover in the name of family respectability. In the opera, Rodolfo playfully promises Mimì that he will buy her a beautiful necklace if he inherits a fortune from his 'zio milionario' (millionaire uncle), but Puccini and his librettists declined to develop the subject further, recognising that the plot device had become something of a cliché. This omission came as a relief to some of the critics, who already discerned a resemblance between *La bohème* and *La traviata* that was rather too close for comfort. *The New York Times* reported in 1898: 'Here is Rodolfo, a poverty-stricken poet, who wears very bad clothes and—Heaven be praised—has no "Di Provenza" father' (a reference to the aria 'Di Provenza il mar, il suol', sung by the character Germont in Verdi's opera).[6]

La bohème's central tragedy needs no helping hand from the presence of a quasi-pantomime villain in the form of a spurned admirer or domineering father. Rather, it is brought about by sheer bad luck. Rodolfo and Mimì are a young, poor couple in love for whom life simply gets in the way. The reasons for their separation are mundane: petty jealousy, financial considerations, and above all a young man's fear of responsibility. It is worth reminding ourselves, incidentally, that although Puccini and his librettists address a variety of different types of love in the opera, it is specifically *young* love that they celebrate. All of the older lovers in the opera are presented as faintly ridiculous. The landlord Benoît is mocked by the Bohemians for his age, his inappropriate romantic indiscretions, and his fantasies about buxom women. Alcindoro, Musetta's elderly lover, is an absurdly servile figure whom she treats like a pet dog and humiliates by flirting openly with Marcello.

La bohème is unusual, in operatic terms, in the way in which it presents a romantic relationship, perfectly capturing the *coup de foudre* of a fortuitous chance encounter, yet also acknowledging the pragmatic complexities of making a relationship work in difficult circumstances. The way in which Puccini treats the experience of falling in love is worthy of note. Whereas in operas of the earlier nineteenth century, the duet where the two lovers meet is essentially 'just another duet', the expanded compositional techniques available to composers by the 1890s in terms of scenic organisation meant that Puccini was able to 'mark off' the love scene from the preceding music as something distinctly different, making it stand out in relief from the surrounding music, to considerable dramatic effect. (This is a technique he would develop further in his later operas, where the deliberate contrast between moments of lush lyricism and the increasingly compositionally adventurous music surrounding them became even more pronounced.[7])

The first-act love scene temporarily changes *La bohème*'s sense of musical and dramatic pacing. The opera is, for the most part, relentlessly fast-moving, but the lyrically expansive section towards the end of Act 1 where Rodolfo and Mimì meet and introduce themselves—not only to the audience but to each other—represents the only comparatively static moment in the work, bar its *dénouement*. The effect of this slowing down of dramatic tempo is threefold. Returning to the idea of the opera as a succession of contrasts, this sequence provides some respite from the hectic music that precedes and follows it. More pragmatically, it satisfied the desire of both Puccini's audience and his money-minded publishers for detachable set pieces that could be milked for profit beyond the opera house. But most importantly, this moment of lush lyricism— super sweet, almost overwhelming us with emotion in the way in which Puccini stacks three 'big tunes' back to back ('Che gelida manina', 'Sì, mi chiamano Mimì', 'O soave fanciulla')—effectively captures the dramatic intensity of the moment. Precisely because of the contrast with the hectic music surrounding it, this sequence encapsulates the way in which two new lovers become completely wrapped up in the moment: time seems, effectively, to stand still. But, of course, the whole message of the opera is that time is ultimately unstoppable, so the pace will pick up again soon enough.

There is an innocence to Puccini's depiction of love in *La bohème* that contrasts with how he treats the subject elsewhere. This is not the heated passion of *Manon Lescaut*, whose Act 2 love duet presents the reunion of Manon and Des Grieux at Geronte's apartment as visceral, angry, and fevered. The twists and turns of the conversation between this pair—here breathless and confused ('Tu, tu amore tu'), there commanding and determined ('Taci, taci')—is a brilliant depiction of a couple in the grip of an obsession. And by the time we reach the section beginning 'O tentratrice', the languorous eroticism of the scene (the voices underpinned by impassioned string playing) is plain for all to hear, however conservative a production may be at the visual level. In *Madama Butterfly*, similarly, the wedding-night love duet is surely one of the most vivid depictions of the act of love-making at the purely musical level, leaving little to the imagination with its rising lines, its ebbing and flowing. The way in which Puccini plays with the listener, withholding harmonic resolution across a prolonged period of some fifteen minutes, is surely a not-so-subtle homage to the famously erotic love duet from Wagner's *Tristan und Isolde*.

La bohème does not depict love in such hot-blooded terms, not least because we are invited to believe that Rodolfo and Mimì's relationship is of a more serious and sweet nature than that between Manon and Des Grieux or that between Butterfly and Pinkerton. The love music here is for the most part more sober, more tentative. However, great depth of feeling is expressed by moments of fervour that well up here and there, as if apparently from nowhere, and subside back into the musical texture. The vocal line ascends, the tempo becomes more expansive, the dynamics swell to a *forte* or *fortissimo*, and the strings in octaves double the voices. We encounter this technique in both characters' opening arias: Rodolfo's account of his artistic dreams (explaining that hopes, dreams, and castles in the air make him a millionaire in spirit) and Mimì's exuberant, luxuriant explanation in her introductory aria of how winter gives way to spring ('ma quando vien lo sgelo, il primo sole è mio, il primo bacio dell'aprile è mio!'). We hear it again in Rodolfo's ardent and desperate admission in Act 3 of his inability to hide his feelings (the passage commencing 'In van, in van nascondo, la mia vera tortura').

Rodolfo and Mimì's relationship may seem idealised on the face of it but is actually far from perfect. Rodolfo has a bizarrely irrational jealous streak. When wandering around the Latin Quarter with Mimì in an apparently blissful state at their newly found love, he suddenly reprimands her for looking at other men, an accusation prompted simply by her spotting a group of students. His words at this point are, Puccini's performance directions tell us, merely 'playful', and yet in the Café Momus, in a highly seductive melodic line, he suddenly warns Mimì that he will not forgive her if provoked as Musetta provokes Marcello. Between Acts 2 and 3 the relationship between Rodolfo and Mimì seems to have turned rather more dysfunctional: Mimì tells Marcello at the Barrière d'Enfer that Rodolfo's suspicions provoke him to anger and rage ('he shouts at me all the time'). The violence of what is being implied here is easy to overlook, accompanied as these words are by Puccini's aforementioned impassioned style (high vocal notes, crescendo, string doubling at the octave). But might there be a potentially rather shocking nexus of love and anger being established here?

Arman Schwartz has gone so far as to portray Rodolfo as a narcissistic bully.[8] He notes that Rodolfo introduces himself using heroic musical language and grandiose words, whereas Mimì's corresponding introduction is more hesitant and concerned with her humdrum day-to-day routine. Rodolfo is 'a poet', Mimì just 'your neighbour'. In Schwartz's reading, Rodolfo is not so much a caring lover, or even an equal partner, as a controlling egotist who refuses to let go of Mimì's hand, spies on her when she is sleeping, and exhibits paranoid tendencies. (The creators of *The Simpsons* picked up on Rodolfo's self-centred tendencies in a skit in which Homer Simpson, incongruously hired to sing the role and suffering from a bad back, throws the dead Mimì out of bed, gets in himself and cries, 'Me me!'[9])

But is Schwartz's interpretation going too far? Is Rodolfo really some sort of tyrant or merely an immature young man who cannot cope with the challenging circumstances in which he finds himself? In his own passionate outpouring to Marcello, he chastises himself for his inability to provide Mimì with the comfortable, warm home she needs for her recovery. And the moments in the opera where Rodolfo shows anger are vastly overwhelmed by those in which he shows Mimì the most touching tenderness. Different performances will play up different nuances, of course, but there is something rather dispiriting about the prospect of an interpretation in which Rodolfo becomes a really nasty piece of work, and Mimì yet another silly, pitiable woman who has fallen for a bad man. These are flawed individuals. There are few operatic moments as profoundly human as that in Act 3 where Rodolfo is sarcastic and bitter about Mimì and Marcello responds with words that in modern parlance might translate as 'You don't sound like you mean it, mate', leading the emotional floodgates to open. If we cannot believe in the sincerity of

PUCCINI'S *LA BOHÈME*

the central relationship, the opera rather loses its *raison d'être*.

Marcello also spends much of his time consumed by jealousy, the difference being, of course, that Musetta really is an incurable flirt and responds to him by giving as good as she gets. He complains about his girlfriend from the first act to the fourth, although finally comes to see her inner kindness. In fact, within the first few pages of the opera, he and Rodolfo are grumbling about men being the victims of women, likening love to a fire in which the man (the kindling) is burnt in an instant and the woman (the spark) stands and watches. This emphasis on the themes of jealousy and untrustworthy women perhaps tells us something about the context in which the opera was produced: a hot-headed Latin culture in which any suggestion of female infidelity could lead to drastic reprisals (as exhibited in other works of the same decade, such as *Pagliacci*). Indeed, sexual jealousy is a recurring theme in Puccini's works: think of *Manon Lescaut, Il tabarro*, and (in a rare variant where it is the woman who is jealous) *Tosca*.

But Marcello and Rodolfo don't seem to exhibit the same misogyny as the vengeful protagonists of some of these other works. Early in Act 4, mirroring the moment in Act 1 where they had complained about unreliable, controlling women, the two men sing the most rueful, heartfelt duet about how much they miss their girlfriends. Moreover, Marcello and Musetta's incessant squabbling followed by reconciliation is a performance, a routine that is played again and again, as is made clear by Schaunard's remark as the two reunite at the end of 'Quando m'en vo' that 'Siamo all'ultima scena' ('We've reached the final tableau!'). There is something universal going on here. A couple hurling insults at each other in the street as Musetta and Marcello do in Act 3—neatly counterpointed with Rodolfo and Mimì's calmer, more pragmatic discussion of separation—could be found nowadays in any city centre on any Saturday night of the year.

La bohème is also striking in the way in which it extends its focus *beyond* the central romance. Depictions of close friendship, as opposed to romantic love, are rather rare in opera, although the homo-social bonds of male communities are explored in works such as *Don Carlos*, *Simon Boccanegra*, and *Otello*. *La bohème* focuses upon a network of friends, shining a spotlight upon the male flatmates initially but later addressing how men and women interact. The friends are also essential to the development of the central romance: they are present on that first night (Marcello's words about poetry even intrude from offstage into the beginning of the love duet) and they help Mimì and Rodolfo to reconcile after their falling out. Musetta brings Mimì to the garret in Act 4, and all the friends are together at the opera's end (in sharp contrast with *La traviata*, where Violetta has been abandoned by her glittering social set).

Within the group, individual characters are carefully distinguished from one another and secondary characters are given their cameo moments. (Musetta has her waltz song; Colline his farewell to his coat.) The opera's status as an ensemble piece, with four male friends who are distinguished musically and dramatically from one another and two contrasting couples, allowed Puccini and his librettists to create different 'types' in order to appeal to the largest possible audience and to create bonds of identification. The fact that Puccini was explicitly thinking in such terms is demonstrated by his remark to Illica from his country retreat that he was 'at grips with our types'.[10] The male viewer could playfully choose which of Puccini's four Bohemians he most resembled; likewise, a female audience member might see herself reflected in either the sweet, good-hearted Mimì—literally the girl next door—or her sassier and more high-spirited friend Musetta. So successful was this device of creating character archetypes that it was widely adopted into popular culture. Indeed, it was still being imitated a century later by the creators of television comedies (think of the television series *Friends*, with its depiction of twenty-something relationships in an urban loft setting) and pop bands (The Spice Girls, who were explicitly, and cynically, labelled as particular types for fans to emulate).

In another departure from the nineteenth-century operatic tradition, a noteworthy aspect of Puccini's operas in general is the unheroic nature of his male characters, with the exception of Dick Johnson in *La fanciulla del West*. *La bohème* conforms to this rule: Rodolfo is vulnerable and ultimately paralysed by weakness. But the world in which the opera takes place is a rather masculine one, albeit not a macho one. Large stretches of the opera are dominated by male voices and male concerns, but these are sensitive, artistic men (a notable feature of their domestic life is a propensity for breaking into spontaneous dance). The conversations in the first act are by turns trivial, profound, blokey, sensitive, and downright bizarre. As the conversation proceeds, it meanders from Musetta's flightiness to fantasies about food, wine, and cigars. Schaunard's surreal story about being asked to play music until a parrot dies gives way to the friends' mischievous coaxing of Benoît to reveal his adulterous encounters.

This is very different terrain from the many Puccini operas—most notably *Madama Butterfly*—in which a strong female character is the principal focus of our interest and empathy, and the subject matter entirely serious. In dramatic terms, *La bohème*'s women function mainly in terms of their relationship to the men, as different types of love interest. This was typical of nineteenth-century representations of the Bohemian life (see also George Du Maurier's *Trilby*, whose reception—as we shall see later—became intertwined with that of Puccini's opera). Luc Sante argues that during this period 'Women were affiliated with bohemia, either as accessories, such as the original of Murger's Mimi, a maker of lace and artificial flowers named Lucille Louvet; or occasionally as inspirations'.[11] Both women appear to have a certain degree of independence, yet are ultimately dependent upon men. Mimì supports herself by working but is eventually (if only briefly) forced to take up with a rich protector; Musetta is even more overtly the plaything of a rich sugar daddy.

The friendship between Mimì and Musetta is less well fleshed-out than that between the male Bohemians. Nevertheless, the two female protagonists are sharply differentiated from each other. In the original literary source, the contrast between the two women is far less distinct: Murger's Mimi is fickle and unfaithful, but he also creates a softer, consumptive character called Francine, and Puccini's librettists amalgamated the two. The resulting operatic character was so idealised—potentially, some might argue, to the point of blandness—that Giacosa and Illica noted in the preface to their libretto that her name 'should be, not Mimì, nor Francine, but "The Ideal" '.[12]

Musetta's role in La bohème, meanwhile, was significantly scaled back from that initially envisaged by Illica. The opera was originally to have included an additional 'courtyard act' between Acts 3 and 4, set at an outdoor party thrown by Musetta, at which Mimì would elope with a protector.[13] Even in her reduced version, however, the feisty Musetta is in many ways a more interesting and complex character than Mimì, because of her inherent contradictions. She is simultaneously lacking in morality (by the conventional standards of the day) and ultimately God-fearing. She might seem the epitome of self-confidence, winding men around her little finger, yet spends almost all of Act 2 obsessing about whether Marcello is looking at her and is arguably every bit as needy as him or Rodolfo. Her aria 'Quando m'en vo', meanwhile, is all about being looked at and the pleasure of being looked at by strangers on the street—often sung, moreover, while sprawled on a table or standing atop a bar. The question of whether this is an expression of female empowerment or the ultimate representation of woman as constructed through the male gaze is a moot point.

Although both roles are for soprani, Mimì and Musetta are differentiated from one another in their musical language, notably in the ways in which they are first presented to us. Mimì's self-presentation to Rodolfo ('Si, mi chiamano Mimì') is slow and lyrical and seems remarkably muted and modest, coming as it does immediately after his grandiose, passionate aria about poetry and love. Musetta's language when we first encounter her in Act 2 is jerky, fragmented, and nervy, often staccato and leaping all over the register. That is, until she goes into premeditated seduction mode for 'Quando m'en vo', a waltz with long, languorous lines and far more stepwise motion. Unlike Mimì's aria, which is simply the character expressing herself, this is a conscious 'performance': diegetic music, which is to say music that it is heard by the other characters not as speech but as a song. (Indeed, it is evidently her signature piece: we hear a fragment of her singing the same melody in the tavern in Act 3.) The two women's different attitudes towards their men is neatly encapsulated at the end of this aria when Musetta sings a high G minim, followed by a crotchet on the G an octave lower, and Mimì copies. Musetta's words here are 'Vinto!' (the conclusion of the line 'Marcello è vinto!', 'Marcello is conquered'), whereas Mimì's are 'T'amo!' ('I love you').

The strategy of presenting two very different female types in a single opera was, of course, a tried and tested one: the contrast could not be sharper, for example, in the case of the earthy, sexy mezzo Carmen and the whiter-than-white soprano Micaëla, who embodies the nineteenth-century 'angel in the house' archetype to such an extent that she is closely identified in the libretto with Don José's mother. But *La bohème* is striking for the fact that Mimì and Musetta are friends, rather than the more standard romantic rivals so often pitted against each other in opera. Over and over again, *La bohème* is an opera that pushes at convention, that is almost deliberately 'unoperatic'. The same applies to the opera's treatment of death.

DEATH AND NOSTALGIA

Opera is often mocked for its representation of death: numerous are the far-fetched or downright absurd operatic death scenes, and in the earlier nineteenth century it was standard practice for characters to continue to sing for a lengthy period after receiving a fatal wound. Verdi's *La traviata* was one of the first operas to present a death from natural causes; *La bohème* goes a step further in its realism and is striking even within the context of Puccini's own oeuvre. Mimì's demise is quiet, quick, and unobtrusive: the precise moment of departure is signalled to the audience by a B minor triad in the orchestra but goes unnoticed by the other characters as they become caught up in their own personal anguish. Yet despite the 'modernity' of Mimì's death in this sense, Illica and Giacosa still adhered to certain conventions of the typical nineteenth-century literary death scene, where the protagonist often dies in a familiar, cherished place, surrounded by comforting objects, and in the company of loved ones (figure 1.2).

The unassuming treatment of death here underlines the fact that the passing away of a Parisian seamstress from consumption would have seemed a fairly unremarkable event at the time when the opera was set, when the disease was rife in urban centres. Yet it is the contrast between the sheer ordinariness of the event and the personal tragedy it becomes for Rodolfo that arguably makes this one of the most affecting of operatic deaths. It was a death scene that was, on the whole, praised by critics of the day. The critic for the French newspaper *Le XIX siècle*, for example, called it 'one of the most moving and well-presented things that

FIGURE 1.2   Scene from Act 4 of the opera *La bohème* by Giacomo Puccini
(1858–1924) (b/w photograph) / Civica Raccolta Stampe Bertarelli,
Milan, Italy / Bridgeman Images.

we have seen in the theatre for a long time', while for *The London Daily News* it was touching and genuinely dramatic but 'commendably brief'.[14]

Some more recent commentators have recoiled from the reaction Mimì's death often prompts. Lindenberger, for instance, writes with a perceptible shudder that 'Even the most routine performances of *La bohème* and *Madama Butterfly* set off conspicuous outbursts of tears as spectators witness the heroines' deaths'.[15] This, as it happens, was precisely the point: sentiment was considered paramount in nineteenth-century Italian opera and moving the listener to tears was a primary objective. But one might argue that it is not so much Mimì's death itself that moves us as the reaction of the other characters to it: the way in which they fuss around, not knowing what to do with themselves; the appalled awkwardness of the Bohemians who realise what has happened before Rodolfo does; Rodolfo's own final anguished cry of 'Mimì.' Characters who normally express themselves in song suddenly revert to speech, the loss of their musical voices symbolising their powerlessness to help.[16]

The opera *has* to end with Mimì's death, because—to put it glibly—a tragic opera wouldn't be an opera if the heroine survived. But it is also dramatically necessary on another level. In Murger's play it is clear that Rodolphe regards his lover's death as representing the end of his own youth: the play ends with the line: 'Oh my youth, it is you they are burying!' ('O ma jeunesse, c'est vous qu'on enterre!').[17] In Giacosa's and Illica's libretto, as Mimì nears her end, Rodolfo reflects wistfully upon the happier times now past and sings 'Oh! Mimì, how brief my youth was!' ('Ah! Mimì, mia breve gioventù!'). And other characters also reflect on the fragility of youth: even Marcello, driven to distraction by Musetta's provocations in Act 2, is compelled to cry out, 'My youth, you're still alive, your memory is not dead . . .' ('Gioventù mia, tu non sei morta, né di te morto è il sovvenir').

Nostalgia is everywhere in Puccini's operas. We might point, for example, to Manon Lescaut yearning for her days with Des Grieux in 'In quelle trine morbide', or to Rinuccio and Lauretta reflecting on their first kiss in the hills of Fiesole as they turn to the panoramic vista of Florence at the end of *Gianni Schicchi*. Then there is Butterfly's wait for Pinkerton's return—played out with the most agonising slowness—as she clings desperately to his casual remark about returning when the robin builds its nest again. As we can see, then, this is not merely a yearning for eras past but a specific nostalgia for the blossoming of youthful love affairs, often now in jeopardy. Thus, at the end of *La bohème*, Mimì and Rodolfo constantly remind each other—both through music and text—of the moment of their coming together. As Musetta recounts discovering her friend almost dead with exhaustion, and subsequently as Mimì says that she feels better and being back in the apartment makes her happy, the orchestra plays various themes from her Act 1 aria. An instrumental interlude as Schaunard and Colline depart and Mimì pretends to sleep reprises the central theme from the love duet 'O soave fanciulla' ('Ah! Tu sol commandi amor'). Even though winter has given way to spring, Mimì's tiny hands are frozen once again, but she feels happiness as she thinks back to the olden days, affectionately quoting Rodolfo's 'Che gelida manina'.

Nostalgia might seem an innocuous enough concept, but from the nineteenth century onwards it came to be regarded as something rather suspect in intellectual circles, since it is but a short leap from nostalgia to sentimentality. As Kunio Hara summarises in his extended study of nostalgia in Puccini's operas, the word took on 'a decidedly negative connotation as a sentimental, indulgent, and trivial yearning for the objects or conditions of the past'.[18] Thus, Puccini's concern with the theme of nostalgia became a significant factor in the critical denigration of his oeuvre as emotionally manipulative. At the same time, of course, nostalgia is fundamental to that oeuvre's success, and to the popularity of *La bohème* in particular. Nostalgia for a first love, for lost loves, and for carefree, youthful optimism is something to which everyone can relate. (As the author of a British 1940s opera appreciation manual wrote, '*La bohème* is a testament of youth. For that reason it is an opera one finds very difficult to criticise and almost impossible not to love'.[19]) One can, of course, also feel nostalgic for places and indeed for places in certain periods of history—even if one wasn't personally there.[20] It is to this subject—Puccini and his librettists' construction of a romanticised 'old' Paris that tapped into their audience's fantasies—that I shall now turn.

P ARIS: CITY OF LIGHT, CITY of love. The French capital seems—both in itself and because of the symbolism it has accrued through countless cultural representations, high and low—to be bound up inextricably with *La bohème*. It is hard to imagine more quintessentially Parisian locations than those that form the backdrop for Puccini's opera: the Latin Quarter, the starving artist's garret, the pavement café. In this chapter I shall argue that Puccini's opera was not only shaped by the city's mythologisation but actively contributed to it. Yet, as we shall see, the relationship between *La bohème* and Paris was not as straightforward as it might at first appear.

Puccini's operas, set in locations as varied as Rome (*Tosca*), Nagasaki (*Madama Butterfly*), and a California

Puccini's La bohème. Alexandra Wilson, Oxford University Press (2021). © Oxford University Press.
DOI: 10.1093/oso/9780190637880.001.0001.

mining town (*La fanciulla del West*)—with brief excursions to the French Riviera (*La rondine*) and somewhere barren in Louisiana (*Manon Lescaut*)—offered Italian theatregoers of his era the opportunity to indulge in a sort of vicarious operatic tourism. It is easy to see a parallel here with the way in which the new illustrated magazines of the turn of the century employed the medium of photography to open up previously little-known exotic locales to an Italian readership; Puccini's works were, as it happens, promoted in the very same publications. But of all the locations that Puccini 'visited' in his operas, Paris was the one to which he would return most frequently. He depicted the city four times across the course of his career, in *Manon Lescaut* (1893), *La bohème* (1896), *La rondine* (1917), and *Il tabarro* (1918). Although these four operas are set in different historical periods that moved progressively closer to Puccini's present (respectively the late eighteenth century, around 1830, the mid nineteenth century, and 1910), there are strands of intertextual connection between them. *La rondine*, like *La bohème*, deals with transient romances in Parisian social spaces among the not quite respectable. *Il tabarro*, meanwhile, though more contemporary in focus than *La bohème*, continues the theme of Parisian poverty. This opera even features a street singer who sings a ballad about Mimì and quotes a motif from *La bohème*, a knowing touch that shows the extent to which Puccini himself was aware of the way in which his earlier opera had contributed to the city's mythologisation. Extramarital love affairs in a city tolerant of such freedoms are common to all four works.

Puccini's fascination with Paris is not surprising when we consider that late nineteenth-century Italy was in the grip of a fever for all things French. French books in translation were very much in vogue, in part because Italy did not have a strong novelistic tradition of its own. (The poet Giosuè Carducci went so far as to write in 1894 that 'in literature we have become a French *département*'.[1]) Several late nineteenth-century Italian painters relocated to Paris, or visited the city regularly.[2] Some of their artworks picked up explicitly on French stylistic influences and introduced them to Italian audiences: Federico Zandomeneghi's *Al Caffè Nouvelle Athènes*, for example, recalls Manet's *Un bar aux Folies Bergère*.

The theatrical repertory in *fin-de-siècle* Italy was also dominated by translations of crowd-pleasing French boulevard dramas. Even on the operatic stage, French works were pushing the native repertory to one side: the Sonzogno publishing house, rival to Ricordi, spotted a commercial opportunity in the 1860s for the promotion of popular French operas and operettas. Italian composers jumped upon the bandwagon for all things French: Puccini's and Leoncavallo's versions of *La bohème* were merely the latest in a succession of Parisian-set operas to grace the Italian operatic stage in the last decade of the nineteenth century. Eighteenth-century Paris was a particular font of creative imagination for the young composers of the era, inspiring not only the passionate second act of Puccini's own *Manon Lescaut* but Revolutionary-themed operas such as Umberto Giordano's *Andrea Chénier*, as well as the later *Adriana Lecouvreur* (Francesco Cilea, 1902) and *Il piccolo Marat* (Mascagni, 1921).

Looking further back, Paris is, of course, the primary setting for *La traviata*, in which the corrupt, morally bankrupt city is contrasted with the bucolic French countryside, site of thwarted happiness. Verdi spent several years living in Paris during the 1850s with his mistress Giuseppina Strepponi. Three decades later, Leoncavallo immersed himself in the Bohemian life, playing the piano at Parisian café-concerts and using the experience as a stimulus for his opera *Zazà* (1900). For Puccini, as we shall see, the connection to the French capital was one step further removed.

AN IMAGINARY PARIS?

It is a truism that Puccini, who considered himself first and foremost a 'man of the theatre', found the concept of geographical ambience an important creative stimulus. Puccini's biographers have repeatedly argued that he was scrupulous about researching the specific atmosphere and sound worlds of the locations in which his operas were set, either by visiting them in person or, in the case of more distant locales, by seeking out advice from those in the know. Most famously, he explored Rome at dawn when writing *Tosca* to note the precise pitches of the matins bells. The composer would later become something of a globetrotter, promoting his operas and assisting with their first performances in both North and South America. It therefore comes as a surprise to learn that he had not actually visited Paris at the time of writing *La bohème*, and more interesting still is the fact that he does not appear to have felt the *need* to go there, despite the comparatively short distances involved. Puccini was, indeed, reportedly amazed that Leoncavallo had travelled to soak up the atmosphere of the Latin Quarter at first hand.[3] He would eventually visit Paris in

1897, en route home from the British première of *La bohème* in Manchester, and he returned the next year to supervise the French première at the Opéra Comique.

It is worth remembering that the Paris depicted by Murger was not, in any case, the Paris Puccini would have encountered had he cared to make the journey prior to composing his opera. Rather, this was a story set, at least ostensibly, in a Paris that had already been swept away by Baron Haussmann in his regeneration programme of the 1850s and 1860s. Murger's Paris—known by the late nineteenth century as 'old Paris'—was for the most part no longer there to see, except through a booming trade in postcards and prints aimed at tourists, which could just as easily be accessed from afar. Furthermore, it must surely have been clear, including to Puccini and his librettists, that Murger's depiction of a charmingly poverty-stricken city was a nostalgic, sentimental construction, stylised so as to appeal to contemporary middle-class taste. In short, the Paris that Puccini had to recreate in his opera was a Paris of the imagination that everyone already knew; further research was not required.

But there was perhaps another reason why Puccini did not feel the need to visit Paris. Biographers have repeatedly suggested that in his own mind the composer was not really depicting Paris at all, despite the opera's symbolic landmarks. Rather, he was depicting somewhere closer to home: the Milan of his student days.[4] Puccini was at the Conservatorio at precisely the moment when the aforementioned *Scapigliatura* movement was in full swing. In order to construct *La bohème* as a semi-autobiographical work, Puccini's biographers have referred repeatedly to a letter of 1882 in which the young composer asked his uncle to send money to help him buy a stove and coal to heat his digs. Further ammunition has been added to the legend by the fact that the first theme we hear in the opera—which recurs as that of the Bohemians—is based on one of Puccini's own student compositions, the *Capriccio sinfonico*.

Simple comparisons between art and life demand scrutiny, of course. Attempts to situate *La bohème*'s action in the Milan of the composer's youth were clearly part of a stereotypical rags-to-riches mythology that was built up across the course of and after his lifetime. (Interestingly, this narrative simultaneously undermined the one about his supposed obsession with geographical authenticity, but the contradiction is rarely if ever noted.) The idea of Puccini as a Bohemian was one that was widely perpetuated by his friends and supporters: see, for example, the title of Dante Del Fiorentino's 1952 book *Immortal Bohemian: An Intimate Memoir of Giacomo Puccini*.[5] But perhaps the reason why even the more astute Puccini biographers do not dismiss such theories as romantic hagiography is because Puccini seems to have bought into the fantasy himself by cultivating a Bohemian persona even once he was wealthy and successful—at least out of the public eye.

In 1894 the composer and friends established a Bohemian club in a hut near his writing retreat on the banks of Lake Massaciuccoli, at the foot of the Apuan Alps. A number of painters affiliated with the Macchiaioli school lived locally. Puccini invited artistic friends old and new to join him in eating and drinking well and playing schoolboy pranks. Biographer Michele Girardi writes that this social milieu, among idealistic albeit none-too-successful artists, was significant to the conception of *La bohème*: 'For Puccini, the well-to-do artist still susceptible to memories of his immediate past, it was like having a live model for his drama, a slice of life ready to be wrapped in music'.[6] The composer became particularly friendly with the painter Ferruccio Pagni, who claimed to be the real Colline, and who explains in his memoirs that another member of the group, Francesco Fanelli, was Marcello, with Puccini himself as Rodolfo.[7]

This element of role-play, of playing at and even dressing up as Bohemians, would, incidentally, be a factor not only in the work's genesis but in its performance and its reception. For example, Savva Mamontov, the impresario who first staged *La bohème* in Russia, encouraged his singers to visit Paris and immerse themselves in the Bohemian lifestyle in preparation for performing the piece; one spoke of having 'made friends with the real Rodolfo and Marcello'.[8] Meanwhile, in the memoirs of the little-remembered British novelist Thomas Burke, which focus on the artistic community in London before the First World War, we read about a manufactured Bohemia in Chelsea where pretentious young people dressed up as characters from Murger's novel and Puccini's opera.[9]

Within Puccini's lifetime, the argument that the composer was 'really' depicting Milan or taking inspiration from a small hamlet in rural Tuscany was also in part a strategy to deflect criticism the composer attracted for repeatedly choosing to set non-Italian subjects. Throughout his career, Puccini encountered hostility from critics who believed him to be betraying his national heritage by setting operas in foreign locations, a curious argument given that Verdi's works had only occasionally been Italian in setting. These comments need to be viewed within the context of a bigger charge of internationalism that would dog Puccini throughout his career—increasingly so with his twentieth-century works—not only in terms of subjects set but in terms of musical language and writing works for foreign theatres.

Critics differed in opinion about the extent to which the music sounded French. A correspondent for the British periodical *The Stage* argued in 1899 that, despite the ostensibly Parisian setting necessary for the Bohemian subject matter, the music itself was thoroughly Italian:

> The characters have their nationality played with and disposed of in true opera style. As a basis for the plot they essentially should be Parisian—there is no Latin Quarter outside Paris; but they all are influenced by Puccini's music, which belongs to the later Italian school, of which he, Leoncavallo and Mascagni are worthy heads. They bear the stamp of an Italian's conception of their temperament. However, these are failings inseparable from grand opera and are made acceptable in the company of the composer's graceful melody.[10]

In contrast, it is interesting to observe some French critics arguing that the music *did* sound French, G. Salvayre of *Gil Blas*, for example, arguing that the music seemed barely Italian at all. Puccini had inherited virtually nothing from his great musical ancestors and his harmonic language was on a more sophisticated plane than that of his *verismo* contemporaries. The biggest influence that this critic (and others after him) identified was not Verdi but Massenet.[11] (One critic considered the influence a regrettable one, since it appeared to have placed limitations on Puccini's spontaneity: the Act 1 love duet was, he claimed, too similar to the love duet in *Werther*.[12]) Alfred Bruneau—himself a composer, who collaborated with Émile Zola on a number of French realist operas—also detected the strong Massenet influence, while simultaneously hearing Puccini's score as 'absolutely Italian' in its motifs, harmonies, and orchestration.[13]

It is, of course, rather hard to pin down exactly what might constitute 'French'-sounding music in any case. Puccini's opera is not musically specific to its locale in the way Giordano's *Andrea Chénier* attempts to be, with its incorporation of French Revolutionary songs, although one might argue that we hear a distant echo of such a sound-world in the band music of *La bohème*'s second act (the one most concerned with creating local colour). Some of Puccini's more outspoken critics have questioned whether the supposedly distinctive sense of place in Puccini's works is at all convincing from the musical point of view. But Richard Specht, writing in the 1930s, surely went too far in arguing that the music in *La bohème*, *Tosca*, *Fanciulla*, *Il tabarro*, and *La rondine* 'might easily be interchanged with one another and would suit the different dramatic situation equally well, or equally badly'.[14]

The idea that *La bohème* might just as easily be set in Milan as in Paris also plays into a broader debate about the disputed location of Bohemia. Murger—in common with many other commentators—is said to have asserted that 'the real Bohemian could exist only in Paris'.[15] Yet Vincent Seligman argued in the 1930s that Puccini and Leoncavallo had found Bohemia in Milan and the interwar English intelligentsia in Bloomsbury.[16] Jonathan Rose, writing more recently, asserts that while Bohemia must always be at the heart of a great urban centre—'a suburban Bohemia seems a contradiction in terms, even an obscenity'—it could just as easily be in Greenwich Village as on the Parisian *rive gauche*.[17] Bohemia was, in fact, more a state of mind, a way of dressing and behaving, than an actual place, arguably just as idealised as any 'exotic' operatic locale.[18]

Even if we were to agree that the quintessential Bohemian *milieu* may be found in Paris, we might struggle to pinpoint its exact location within the city. The illusory, imagined nature of this geographical Bohemia is underlined by the fact that the real Café Momus that inspired Murger was in fact located on the right bank rather than the left, on the Rue des Prêtres-Saint-Germain-l'Auxerrois, close to the Louvre (see figure 2.1). Since Murger's time the site of Bohemian Paris has continued to move around. Montmartre at the turn of the twentieth century; Montparnasse in the 1910s and 1920s; the area around Saint-Germain-des-Prés after World War II. *La bohème* has doubtless maintained its currency at least in part because the idea of Bohemian Paris has replayed itself in so many different periods, whether in the time of Toulouse-Lautrec or that of Simone de Beauvoir.

PARIS OLD AND NEW

However meaningful or not Paris really was to Puccini, a stereotypical concept of the city was always going to be fundamental in selling *La bohème* to audiences. But which Paris? Despite the historically scrupulous sets and costumes evoking the 'old' Paris of 1830 used in the first production,

FIGURE 2.1   Rue des Prêtres-Saint-Germain-l'Auxerrois, Paris, 1er
arrondissement (1849) Gallica Digital Library. Wikimedia
Commons. No permission needed.

Puccini's opera tapped into an emerging set of tropes about the 'new' city that were being fashioned in the 1890s. (A British critic noted in 1897 that 'in many instances the scenes might be dated today'.[19]) The opera encapsulated a vision of the French capital that was close to Parisians' own hearts at the turn of the twentieth century, as a collection of village-like neighbourhoods peopled by humble seamstresses, organ grinders, and itinerant salesmen.[20] Such figures are, of course, effectively the cast of Puccini's second act. This is an act where atmosphere and a sense of place—the general hubbub of street life—count more, we might say, than character development (barring the showcasing of Musetta), which is more pronounced in the other acts.[21]

Puccini and his librettists recreated on the stage characters who were familiar literary types that harked back to the early nineteenth century. (As one Parisian critic prefaced his summary of the opera's plot, 'I don't think I need introduce the main characters of *La Vie de bohème*; you already know them'.[22]) At the same time, they were realistic figures that one might—at least in theory—meet on the streets of Paris in the 1890s. This applied to the female leads in particular. The *fin-de-siècle* Parisian tourist industry constructed the good-hearted young *demimondaine* as both symbolic of the city itself and an attraction for visitors. As historian Charles Rearick puts it, 'A specialized publishing industry fed men's fantasies about the city's women, especially about the *petites femmes de Paris*'. Erotic postcards, photos and magazines 'depicted young Parisian women as a type—sexy, light-hearted, and ever-ready for amorous adventure. That was exactly what a host of provincial men as well as foreigners were eager to believe and to find'.[23]

Musetta embodies this archetype most obviously, but even Mimì would plainly have been seen as transgressing norms of decent, bourgeois behaviour to an audience of the 1890s. Audience members of 1896 could, if they so wished, make a quick jaunt to Paris to find a real-life Musetta or a thoroughly modern Mimì. How many actually did is a matter for speculation, but it is an intriguing thought that Puccini's opera might, through its idealisation of Bohemian Paris, have fuelled a type of contemporary sex tourism, or at least one of the imagination. Cinema, of course, still revels in the cliché of Paris as the city to which one travels to 'get the girl' (think, for example, of Woody Allen's 2011 film *Midnight in Paris*).

Puccini and his librettists seized upon specific Parisian spaces that—while far removed from the city's grandest monuments—had already become quintessential emblems of the city by the 1890s: the starving artist's garret and the pavement café. These rather humble manifestations of Parisian life seemed, in a sense, to have the most authenticity in the romantic imagination: they are the *milieux* that every gap-year student still seeks to find today. Michela Ronzani observes that the visual iconography created by Ricordi for the opera's first production homed in not on the opera's most dramatic episodes but rather upon more mundane scenes that emphasised local colour (Benoît coming to collect rent; the four friends dancing; Musetta at the Café Momus) and 'highlighted the intimate, localized atmosphere of the group of friends and their environs in Paris.'[24]

By the time Puccini wrote his opera, travel guides aimed at the international market were already mythologising Paris as a seductive, timeless city.[25] Although many of these concentrated on the city's fashionable and glamorous quarters, they also devoted space to its seedier areas, which maintained a certain picturesque allure. Voyeuristic, thrill-seeking tourists (sometimes accompanied by a detective for protection) could even pay to take guided tours of the city's lowlife quarters: such remnants as still existed of 'old Paris'.[26] Many of the old, poor areas were now in fact gentrified. Pockets of urban poverty certainly continued to exist amidst the glamour of *fin-de-siècle* Paris, although these were often not the areas visited on the tourist trail: rather, the ostensibly down-at-heel places that tourists were taken to were for the most part effectively 'staged'. Turn-of-the-century Paris had created a 'showcase Bohemia', by now centred upon Montmartre's cafés and cabarets, which it exploited for full touristic and commercial effect.[27] All of this was in full swing at the time when Puccini composed *La bohème*. Thus, if Puccini was contributing to an idealised, mythical—but false—representation of Paris, then the Parisians were also at it themselves.

STAGING PARISIAN POVERTY

The more we delve into *La bohème* and its contexts, the more we find the concepts of Paris, poverty, and Bohemianism to be somewhat nebulous—ciphers for a vaguer set of ideas about play-acting, dressing up, and fantasy. This leads us logically to consider how *La bohème*'s artistic representation of urban grittiness plays into this idea of 'stage-set' poverty. It is interesting that many commentators of the 1890s, both in Italy and abroad, expressed relief at the fact that Puccini had not been too crude in his evocation of

Parisian Bohemian life. A correspondent for *The Musical Times* wrote in 1897: 'Bohemian life in the Quartier Latin, or indeed anywhere else, has often its very sordid side, and there is no gainsaying the fact that had Signor Puccini been less of an artist he could have found ample opportunity for emphasising the coarse side of the picture. But from this he has refrained, with wholly satisfying results'.[28]

The *La bohème* subject could plausibly have lent itself to full-on *verismo* treatment, but this was something that Puccini and his librettists resisted. Their representation of Paris is not an entirely pretty one: as Arthur Groos and Roger Parker observe, 'there is an ironic twist, the poet's potentially romantic vista being marred by grey skies and belching smoke'.[29] But ultimately Puccini and his team went even further than Murger had done in romanticising the harsh realities of artistic life in early nineteenth-century Paris. Some of the sterner Parisian critics—going against the grain of the generally positive French reception that the opera received—complained that the work was a superficial fantasy that sacrificed realism. A particular objection was the fact that the characters, one of them stricken with TB, should be living it up outside pavement cafés on a freezing December night, as if it were July.[30] This is picturesque poverty, no socialist message (as called for by Camerone, Murger's Italian translator) intended, or arguably wanted.[31] We are nowhere near the terrain of *verismo* operas such as the scandal-provoking *Mala vita* by Umberto Giordano (1892), about a labourer who tries to reform a prostitute against the backdrop of a squalid Neapolitan slum.

At their most extreme, *verismo* operas were peopled by characters with whom the audience members could, presumably, find few shared experiences: the audience was expected to watch them voyeuristically rather than to empathise with them. But the middle-class audience's ability to feel compassion for the plight of Rodolfo and Mimì, indeed to imagine themselves *as* Rodolfo and Mimì, was a selling-point for the opera from the outset and has continued to be a key factor in its enduring popularity. *La bohème* essentially addresses the well-worn stereotype of the Romantic ideal of the starving artist in the garret, for whom living in squalor is essential, and who would never consider taking a job, since this would mean renouncing one's artistic status. And we are fully aware that it is a stereotype. Puccini's Bohemians, like Murger's, are arguably little more than bourgeois young men playing a game.[32] Their relentless jollity (at least in Acts 1 and 2) in the face of what would in reality have been unremittingly depressing circumstances romanticises their poverty. *La bohème*'s sentimentality also undermines its supposed preoccupation with urban grittiness, creating a work that is more escapism than social critique.

Any impression of realistic poverty has often been further undermined by performance conventions. Take, for example, what singers of the past tended to wear. In the British première in Manchester by the Carl Rosa Company, Alice Esty (Mimì) donned what Puccini's biographer Wakeling Dry called not 'the customary black gown of the little seamstress, but one of some pretensions to magnificence'.[33] And there were reports of Melba following suit at Covent Garden, initially wearing the same plain dress in the first and last acts to emphasise Mimì's continued poverty, but as time went on preferring to wear an elaborate pale blue evening gown and cloak for the final act.[34] The justification—supposedly—lay in Marcello's line at the beginning of Act 4 about having spotted Mimì in a carriage, dressed like a queen. But equally plausible is that such singers were continuing a long nineteenth-century tradition of putting fashion ahead of dramatic verisimilitude, either by substituting their own clothes or demanding extravagant outfits.

There has also always been a tension between the spaces in which the opera is typically performed and the scenes it seeks to depict. The vast stage of a theatre such as the Metropolitan Opera House offers huge creative potential for the realisation of Act 2 and to some extent Act 3 but is surely problematic for Acts 1 and 4. In 1928, Philip Page, a critic for *The London Mercury*, pithily observed in an article entitled 'Realism in Opera' that:

> If the attic in *La bohème* in which Rodolfo and his friends are starving has obviously to be rather larger than a ducal drawing room, the street scene in the next act can look like a street, the café should have real bottles, and the members of that supper party might eat something, be it only sponge-cakes or bananas, instead of picking at empty plates. Operatic snow should look tolerably like snow, instead of resembling post-cards torn in half, fluttering slowly down from the flies.[35]

Page's description paints a wonderful picture of the amateurish staging practices that prevailed in 1920s Britain. But what is particularly interesting in the present context is his reference to the typical garret being 'rather larger than a ducal drawing room', which gets to the nub of an essential paradox about *La bohème*'s supposed verisimilitude. There are various ways of getting around this problem with some creative staging strategies, as we shall see later, but many spectacular garrets live on in major opera houses. Performances in non-conventional spaces such as pubs have allowed the intimacy of the outer acts to shine through, and the audience members to feel as though they are patrons at the Café Momus, though require companies to dispense with an orchestra and anything more than a skeleton chorus. Examples of this mode of presentation include OperaUpClose's touring production, first staged at the Cock Tavern in Kilburn, North London in 2009, and Against the Grain Theatre's production (set in a historic dive bar in Toronto's Annex neighbourhood), which has been performed in bars across Canada since 2011.

Recent productions of *La bohème* have attempted to push it into harsher places, to give it a higher degree of urban realism. We have witnessed numerous gritty *Bohème*s set in nonspecific urban squalor, peopled by drug addicts, prostitutes, and illegal immigrants, which attempt to strip the opera of its perceived sentimentality. Some such productions (discussed in more detail in chapter 5) also move the opera's locale from the *rive gauche* to East London or Brooklyn, often with satisfactory results. But in many productions, even the more adventurous ones, the idea of Paris remains central and is denoted by reference to certain emblematic symbols of the city, particularly in Act 2.

Early productions of the opera typically attempted a forensically realistic representation of the 'old Paris' of prints and sepia photographs. The sets and costumes designed by Lucien Jusseaume for the French première in 1898, for example, drew considerable approval from Parisian critics for their attention to local detail.[36] Numerous directors over the ensuing decades have also striven for historical accuracy. In recent times, however, many directors have dispensed with a strictly period-accurate setting, instead referencing the much-reified Parisian *fin de siècle*, either presented 'straight' or in self-aware fashion. If Murger's Paris had become a nostalgic golden age for audiences of the 1890s, the Paris of the 1890s—*art nouveau* métro entrances and Toulouse-Lautrec's depictions of Montmartre cabarets—has become one in our own age.

Evocations of this aesthetic have been numerous. The second act of the 2017 production directed by Stefano Ranzani for the Teatro La Fenice in Venice was staged against a backdrop of silhouetted buildings (which at first glance appear to be wine bottles) painted with murals advertising absinthe and Le Chat Noir. Davide Livermore's 2012 production for the Opera Company of Philadelphia, meanwhile, created an 'Impressionist' *Bohème*, employing backdrops decorated with fragments from late nineteenth-century paintings, such as Van Gogh's *The Starry Night* and *Sunflowers*, as well as works by Renoir, Cézanne, and other contemporaries. Damiano Michieletto, for the Salzburg Festival of the same year, updated the opera to the present but played out the action of Act 2 against the backdrop of a giant map of the city, the characters stepping around miniature models of Haussmann-era Parisian buildings (see figure 2.2). Finally, Richard Jones, for the Bregenz Festival in 2002, achieved an impressive effect with his recreation of a Parisian café on a floating stage on Lake Bregenz, with giant tables, chairs, and ashtrays and a postcard as backdrop.

FIGURE 2.2   Salzburger Festspiele 2012. Piotr Beczała as Rodolfo and Anna
Netrebko as Mimì in *La bohème*. Photograph by Luigi Caputo.
Wikimedia Commons. No permission needed.

Through its evocation of iconic spaces, the opera and its productions have contributed to a sentimentalised reification of Paris as the 'city of love'. But many of the Parisian references that we find in these productions will play upon audience members' wider understanding of what the city means, drawn from a whole host of pop-culture references. Thus, *La bohème* forms part of a wider association loop, replaying an endless set of Parisian tourist clichés. How far can the constant recycling of the same few tropes go, one wonders? Perhaps it is telling that Claus Guth, the director of the most recent production of the opera to be staged at the Opéra National de Paris itself (2017), decided not to look to the surrounding boulevards for inspiration but to sidestep Parisian imagery altogether and relocate the action to . . . the moon.

CHAPTER 3

LA BOHÈME'S *TRAVELS*

T HE *FIN DE SIÈCLE* was an age of travel, of the cultural
exchange of artworks and ideas on a scale never previously dreamed possible. Although opera had been an
itinerant business almost since its very beginnings, per-
sonnel, works, and even sets and costumes were, by the late
nineteenth century, able to move from country to country
with ever greater ease. This was without doubt an era of
internationalism, for good or ill, and Puccini embraced the
new ethos, looking to the works of foreign contemporaries
for inspiration, travelling around the world supervising
regional premières, and even writing his later operas ex-
pressly for a global audience. (*La fanciulla del West* and *Il
trittico* were first performed at the Metropolitan Opera in
New York; *La rondine*, originally commissioned for Vienna,

Puccini's La bohème. Alexandra Wilson, Oxford University Press (2021). © Oxford University Press.
DOI: 10.1093/oso/9780190637880.001.0001.

ultimately received its première in Monte Carlo.) As time went on, the 'internationalist' label would prove to be both a blessing—in the sense of acclaim and financial gain—and a curse. Some of his contemporaries judged it to be not so much a badge of success as a betrayal of national identity. Within this context, *La bohème*'s transnational peregrinations demand closer attention.

In order to understand the opera's initial reception, it is important to bear in mind the contexts in which it appeared on the stage, and the politico-cultural maelstrom into which it was thrown. Puccini was writing at a moment when Italian opera was perceived to be entering a period of potential crisis, with growing foreign influences taking root in Italy. For example, whereas the repertory at La Scala had been almost entirely home-grown at mid-century, by the 1890s Italian works were being pushed aside by popular French operas and operettas. Wagner's works, meanwhile, posed a significant aesthetic threat, differing so profoundly in musical style, subject-matter, and philosophical intent from the long-established norms of Italian opera and yet enticing a younger generation of composers to turn their backs on tradition and enthusiastically embrace techniques such as through-composition and a more complex use of musical motifs. There was also the pressing need to respond in some way—even if by categorical rejection—to an emerging pan-European musical modernism.

Just as these aesthetic factors would colour the initial reception of *La bohème*, so too would political agendas. Puccini was burdened with a responsibility not only to continue a musical tradition—an expectation that often sat at odds with his personal, rather forward-looking, creative ambitions—but to boost national self-confidence. We might think of the cultural politics of the turn of the twentieth century as a form of aesthetic colonialism, each nation jockeying for pre-eminence and trying to carve out a distinctive identity as the cultural sphere became increasingly internationalised. *La bohème* was first performed only a matter of weeks before the humiliating rout of Italian troops at the Battle of Adwa in Abyssinia (present-day Ethiopia). Italy's attempt at territorial occupation might have been wavering, yet according to critics overcome by the spirit of jingoism, its ability to colonise the world through art lived on—or so they hoped.

Other nations had their own crises of confidence to deal with at this moment of rapid aesthetic change. The German-speaking world, for example, was going through a period of soul-searching about what opera should sound like in the post-Wagnerian era, just as Italy was on a quest for a new cultural hero as Verdi's career drew to its inevitable close. Some of the priorities and preoccupations that shaped the international reception of *La bohème* were shared across borders, and it is fascinating to see the work eliciting similar reactions in cities at a distant remove from one another. On the other hand, some responses were distinctive to their local contexts, and these regional variations are also important to understand. For example, in late nineteenth-century Britain, where the boundaries between high and low art were more fluid than they are generally perceived to be today, opera was regarded as rather frivolous. This contrasted sharply with the situation in Italy or in the German-speaking lands, where opera was treated with the utmost seriousness. In this chapter, I synthesise common strands of response that greeted a selection of premières of *La bohème* on both sides of the Atlantic, before discussing some more unusual early performances that show us ways in which the work was received differently in different contexts.

The first performance of *La bohème* took place at the Teatro Regio in Turin on 1 February 1896, with Cesira Ferrani (previously the first Manon Lescaut) and Evan Gorga in the lead roles. The young Toscanini conducted. Critical responses were mixed: a less-than-ideal cast, with male leads who were either vocally out of sorts or miscast, was part of the problem, although far from the extent of it. A despondent Puccini recalled wandering the backstage corridors of the Teatro Regio overhearing hushed conversations about the mistake he had made and how the opera could not possibly survive long.[1] Ricordi, by contrast, was less troubled by the whispering campaign, or by what the press said the next day: the opera was a sell-out for twenty-four performances in Turin and, in popular terms, a success.[2] The publishing firm swiftly started to rent it to theatres around Italy. *La bohème* encountered some further teething troubles elsewhere: a muted reception in Rome and Naples led Puccini to make some modifications to the score, particularly to Act 2. It was only when the opera crossed the Tyrrhenian Sea to Palermo in April 1896 that it received a wholeheartedly successful reception, with countless curtain calls and an audience that refused to leave the theatre.[3] Thereafter, Puccini's opera would go on to be the hit of the year, leaving the new works by his rivals Leoncavallo (*Chatterton*) and Mascagni (*Zanetto*) trailing far behind.

The international mechanisms for disseminating operas were, by the 1890s, fast and efficient. The Ricordi firm distributed the work around its extensive overseas network, which included all the major European cities and the important operatic outposts of North and South America. (It was Buenos Aires that hosted the first performance outside of Europe, in June 1896, and in 1897 the opera would be performed in cities such as Alexandria, Moscow, Lisbon, Berlin, Rio de Janeiro, and Mexico City.) The publishing house invested heavily in *La bohème*'s promotion, launching a massive publicity campaign centring on Adolfo Hohenstein's simple yet effective poster, across which Puccini's characters, major and minor, spill exuberantly (see figure 3.1). The firm had shops throughout Europe and North and South America selling *La bohème* postcards and themed memorabilia, and used its house journal, the *Gazzetta musicale di Milano*, to promote the work.[4] This strategy undoubtedly helped to propel *La bohème* on its global journey. Nevertheless, in spite of all the advantages Ricordi was able to give Puccini, there were still no guarantees at this early stage of the work securing a firm foothold in the international operatic canon or attracting unanimous critical approval.

CENTRES AND PERIPHERIES

It is worth considering the status of the theatres where the opera was initially performed. Having an opera premiered in Turin was not as much of a coup as having one premiered at La Scala. (Interestingly, it was not until March 1897 that Ricordi would showcase the opera there, despite it being the opera house with which the firm had the closest association.) The Teatro Regio was, nevertheless, a

FIGURE 3.1   Poster for *La bohème*, opera by Giacomo Puccini, 1895 (colour lithograph), Italian School (nineteenth century) / Fondazione Puccini, Lucca, Italy / De Agostini Picture Library / A. Dagli Orti / Bridgeman Images.

top-ranking opera house. Turin was a city renowned for its intellectualism, and there was an openness to forward-looking works and foreign innovations—a frame of reference that would prove challenging for Puccini in unexpected ways. A notable strand in the early performance history of *La bohème*, however, is that as it made its way around the international operatic circuit, it was often performed in secondary theatres and by minor companies that performed in the vernacular. In Vienna, for example, the opera was premiered at the Theater an der Wien—a venue noted for its association with operetta—rather than the more prestigious Hofoper, the reason being that the latter had already booked Leoncavallo's *La bohème*.[5] In Berlin, the opera received its première in June 1897 in German at the Kroll-Oper, while the first Parisian staging was at the Opéra Comique, in French, in June 1898.

But all of these performances were, at least, in capital cities, whereas in some countries the opera was premiered not only in secondary theatres but also in secondary cities. In Russia in January 1897, for example, the opera was given its cautiously received first performance in Moscow—regarded as a cultural backwater compared to the then capital, St Petersburg—and not even at the Bolshoi but the Solodovnikov Theatre. The company that staged it was the Moscow Private Opera, founded by Savva Mamontov, a railway tycoon and patron of the arts.[6]

In Britain, meanwhile, London's Covent Garden Theatre was not willing to take another chance on Puccini, as *Manon Lescaut* had been something of a flop there. Thus, *La bohème* was premiered in April 1897 at the Theatre Royal in Manchester by the Carl Rosa Opera Company, a down-to-earth touring troupe employing British singers to sing in English. To be fair, Manchester was not exactly some out-of-the-way backwater: concert life was thriving there during the Victorian era, thanks largely to the foundation of the Hallé Orchestra. It was also in a sense particularly apposite that *La bohème* should have received its British première in an industrial centre focused upon the garment trade, given the opera's preoccupation with textiles and clothing. (Think of Mimì's status as a seamstress, the nostalgic symbolism of her bonnet from Rodolfo in Act 4, her desire for a hand muff to warm her frozen hands, and Colline's tribute to his old coat.)

But *La bohème*'s first British outing, with the composer in attendance, was far from auspicious: the lead tenor had a heavy cold, other singers struggled with the music, and the English translation was poor. The Carl Rosa took the opera to Covent Garden in October 1897, but it was not performed as part of the glamorous Covent Garden international season until June 1899, when it was sung in Italian by a cast led by Nellie Melba and Fernando De Lucia. Looking back retrospectively thirty years later, Herman Klein identified the British 'Puccini vogue' as only really beginning with this production, where Melba's close association with the role boosted the opera's popularity.[7] Nevertheless, at the time, there was still some doubt about whether the opera would become central to the repertory. The critic for *The Manchester Guardian* wrote: '*La bohème* may never become a permanent favourite with opera-goers; but, rendered as it was last night, the picturesque work will always command hearty acceptance.'[8] Meanwhile, the opera continued to be performed on the touring opera circuit, sometimes to considerable acclaim, sometimes not. In 1899 it suffered the indignity of being labelled 'one of the weakest operas Sheffield has ever heard'.[9]

In the United States, the opera also got off to an inauspicious start. The American première was given in Los Angeles in October 1897 by an ensemble whose name has been variously recorded as the 'Royal Italian Grand Opera' and the 'Milan Royal Opera Company, of La Scala'.[10] The troupe subsequently took the opera to the Wallack's Theatre in New York (a cheap theatre often used for staging melodramas) in May 1898. The ensemble was evidently not as grand as it hoped to sound, and any genuine connection to La Scala was dubious: as *The New York Times* carped, just about every Italian singer claimed to have sung there at some point or another.[11] This production, although heartily applauded by those up in the gallery, was undoubtedly a poor introduction to Puccini's opera for New York audiences, the scratch band of itinerant singers paying 'scant justice' to either the libretto or the score.[12]

Other touring troupes would take a stab at performing *La bohème* in New York over the following months, either legitimately or illegitimately. In October 1898 Ricordi endeavoured unsuccessfully to take legal action against a company that wanted to present the opera at the Casino Theatre on Broadway without securing the necessary rights.[13] The Metropolitan Opera Company took up the opera only in late 1900, performing it first on tour in Los Angeles in November (with Melba and Giuseppe Cremonini as the leads) and at the Metropolitan Opera House itself—then based at the intersection of 39th Street and Broadway—on Boxing Day.[14] As in London, there was little certainty at this stage that the opera would carve out an enduring place in the repertory. William James Henderson of *The New York Times* wrote that 'we cannot believe that there is permanent success for an opera constructed as this one is', notwithstanding its powerful and attractive love music.[15]

BREAKING THE RULES

Puccini's biographer Vincent Seligman argued in the 1930s that 'to their credit it must be said that foreigners generally, and the English in particular, gave [the opera] a far warmer welcome than she had at first known in Italy'.[16] Nevertheless, in none of these cities on either side of the Atlantic can the opera be said to have been an immediate and unanimous critical success, although it was certainly successful from the commercial point of view. Indeed, *La bohème* prompted considerable controversy of one type or another, not least in terms of the way in which it seemed to be flouting operatic norms.

A majority of the critics in Turin responded negatively on the morning after the première, although more favourable reviews appeared as the run progressed. The opera was perceived to be neither corresponding with older Italian traditions nor living up to the new standards being set by forward-looking foreign works. The fact that the latter was even a consideration came down to an accident of timing. Unfortunately for Puccini, the critics who reviewed the first performance of *La bohème* still had *Götterdämmerung* ringing in their ears, a work that had received its Italian première in the same city only a few weeks before.[17] Wagner's music dramas had arrived in Italy belatedly and prompted a sense of shock among many members of the Italian musical establishment, but they were somehow becoming inescapable and, for the more progressive critics, the new yardstick by which all other works should be judged.

William Ashbrook elegantly sums up the jolt the Torinese critics felt in moving in quick succession from Wagner's to Puccini's work thus: '*La bohème* involved a shrinking of aesthetic distance from something as remote as the primeval banks of the Rhine to a smaller-scale world populated by characters one might encounter on the streets of any large city, and it is precisely the adjustment of emotional perspective demanded by Puccini's opera that caused its first audiences to feel they had lost their bearings.'[18] Many critics asserted that they did not consider the lives of students and seamstresses worthy operatic subjects, and argued that operas should deal with significant events rather than simply depicting atmosphere. Puccini's humble protagonists and dramatic concerns should really have come as no shock: *verismo* operas had been flouting expectations about 'proper' operatic subjects for more than half a decade. But finding elements of tragedy and comedy combined in the same work was still an unusual phenomenon. (Historically, the two genres of Italian opera—tragic opera, with nobly born characters, and comic opera, with more humble characters—had been quite separate.)

For the forward-looking Torinese critics, *La bohème*'s orchestration and treatment of thematic material, although innovative in the Italian context, seemed to pale next to Wagner's. The comparison was, of course, an unfair one, since *La bohème* and *Götterdämmerung* aspired to do entirely different things. But the critics became fixated upon the idea of 'organic unity', so fundamental to the Wagnerian aesthetic and found wanting in *La bohème*. Although Puccini's evocative use of reminiscence motifs unified his opera far more tightly than Murger's indisputably episodic novel, the critics could—on a first encounter at least—hear little holding the four acts together.

It was unfortunate for Puccini that Italian listeners, or at least the more learned among them, could not simply accept and assess *La bohème* on its own terms. After all, when the opera was premiered in Paris two years later, the critic for *Le Monde artiste* observed that audiences were perfectly capable of appreciating Vincent d'Indy's esoteric, quasi-Wagnerian *Fervaal* one night and Puccini's entirely different work at the same theatre the next.[19] But the truth of the matter was that Wagner loomed large in *La bohème*'s French reception too. Arthur Pougin, a noted anti-Wagnerian, argued in *Le Ménestrel* that the opera had been so successful not because it was a masterpiece but precisely because it offered light relief for audiences bored by French imitations of Wagner. It contained, he argued, realistic characters who didn't pontificate endlessly through interminable acts, whose actions and feelings audiences could understand, and who expressed themselves in a musical language that was clear, intelligible, and accessible to all.[20] Albert Montel of *Le XIX siècle* concurred that it had taken an Italian composer to give French audiences the emotional sincerity they had been longing for.[21] Ernest Reyer—himself a composer of epic operas, including a *Salammbô* based on Flaubert's novel—noted a certain 'Germanic' sophistication to the orchestration and a few *Leitmotivs* but was relieved that that was the extent of it, since 'We would have been gravely disappointed if an Italian composer hadn't given us an Italian score'.[22]

It is interesting to note that in some national contexts, comparisons with Wagner could be favourable to both composers. An anonymous critic for the *Jornal do Commercio*, a Brazilian newspaper from Rio de Janeiro, observed in 1897 that Puccini had 'found in the German school the tonic that could restore Italian music'.[23] For this commentator, Puccini's 'abandonment of tradition', characterised notably by an amplified, opulent orchestral writing, was not a matter of shame but a positive advance, and not incompatible with the 'eloquent expressiveness' of melody noted elsewhere in this review.

La bohème's structure as a series of incidents or tableaux—its lack of plot, as some saw it—was noted again and again as the opera made its way around the world's stages. In Vienna, in particular, the fact that 'nothing much happens' was deemed a problem. Many critics there felt that Murger's much-loved Bohemian stories simply could not be condensed successfully and that the consequent gaps between the acts meant that episodes lacked psychological logic or conviction. Puccini had done it before, of course, in *Manon Lescaut*, but listeners were still not prepared for this new way of organising an opera.

Similarly, Puccini's attempt to capture realistic conversation struck early reviewers as odd: the libretto had too many words, and in the passages where the Bohemians chatter to one another it was difficult, to ears unused to such musical language, to make out the text. Hanslick complained of 'inexhaustibly garrulous dialogue, which wends its way witlessly, mindlessly around the most everyday things', while the reviewer for the *Wiener Allgemeine Zeitung*—making Puccini's inferiority to Wagner clear—wrote that 'such nervous, asthmatic music has seldom yet been heard . . . This is no longer unending melody; it is unending absence of melody'.[24] Other discerning voices heard things differently, however: the composer Gustav Mahler (who introduced the opera into the repertory of the Hofoper) made a point of noting to a friend that the new opera's music was easy to understand, the orchestration very effective, and the vocal writing admirable.[25]

The perception of *La bohème* as 'tuneless' may seem scarcely believable to our ears, but it was a refrain that returned repeatedly in the early responses. Some of the early Italian critics struggled to make sense of Puccini's distinctively flexible, speech-like musical language, and expressed fearfulness that he was retreating from the nineteenth-century Italian tradition—already somewhat subverted by Verdi—of prioritising the beautiful voice. This was a point of particular concern at the local level, of course, but critics from other countries who lacked a vested interest in the good health of the Italian operatic tradition were also perplexed, the Russian critic Semion Kruglikov observing that 'Despite being a son of a singing nation . . . Puccini is no tune writer. His melody does not possess the free, easy, sincere flow typical of the older Italians'.[26] Given later concerns that Puccini was including detachable arias precisely with one eye on the recording industry, it is ironic that Kruglikov discerned him to be deliberately avoiding melodies on the grounds that '[he] is desperately afraid of clichés, terrified of ending up on a hurdy-gurdy roll'.

Astonishingly, some early listeners heard the opera as not only lacking in melody but also as lacking in emotion. The two complaints were, of course, related in the Italian context, where more conservative critics expected the beautiful voice to reign supreme. This inevitably proved incompatible with the realism that Puccini was seeking in the opera's dénouement and some heard the opera's ending as too calculated and lacking sufficient lyricism. The critic for the Milanese newspaper *Il Secolo*, for example, claimed that the opera did not 'enter the heart', and wished Puccini better luck next time.[27]

Henderson of *The New York Times*, meanwhile, heard Puccini's score as unoriginal, characterised by the sort of 'twistings of rhythm and harmonic disjoinings' that one might find in any of the *verismo* operas that had recently made their way to the States. He questioned the suitability of the music for the action being depicted, beyond the overtly passionate moments in Acts 1 and 3, where Puccini succeeded in striking the right note. Yet the problem for this critic was not so much that Puccini's music was too ugly, but that it was *insufficiently* so: the musical speech was too polished, polite, and pretty to convince, particularly when it came to the colloquial chatter of the Bohemians.[28] Henderson's compatriot Henry Edward Krehbiel of *The New York Tribune* disagreed, writing: 'Sometimes for a moment it is the vehicle of passionate expression, but more often it is the vehicle of noise and sometimes not the vehicle but the sonorous disturbance itself'. This idea was one that would become even more pronounced in the later reception of *Tosca*, but the latter work edges closer to the sonic fabric of *verismo*: to hear *La bohème* dismissed as what we might call 'just noise' is a good deal more surprising. Krehbiel also asserted quite openly that Puccini was 'degrading' music, tapping into a rhetoric of decadence that would become a marked strand in Puccini's twentieth-century reception.

In Vienna, where comparisons between Italian and Germanic styles of composition were inevitably high on the agenda, critics expressed even greater concern about Puccini's lack of respect for the rules, for he had broken some of the defining principles of harmony. Austrian critics repeatedly attacked his tendency to write chains of ascending and descending parallel fifths (as seen at the opening of Act 2 and as Mimì awaits Marcello in Act 3), although they were divided as to whether the cause was incompetence or 'deliberate mischief'. Hanslick was particularly brutal in characterising such passages as 'harmonic atrocities', 'ill-mannered monstrosities', and 'the unmotivated use of the ugly'.[29] There was a similar response in Russia, where the parallel triads and bitonality of Act 2's street scene prompted an outraged critical response.[30] In France, by contrast, many critics seemed relaxed about Puccini's 'offences'. Ernest Reyer of the *Journal des débats* wrote that 'The licences Monsieur Puccini has permitted himself may set the teeth of some of the purists on edge, as when one bites into a green apple: I do not care'.[31] In spite of these few 'peccadilloes', he continued, there were so many exemplary pages in the score that it would be difficult to say that the composer did not know what he was doing.

With the passing of time, such so-called sins would seem comparatively harmless—although musicological textbooks would frown upon them for decades—but the fact that they provoked such outrage upon first hearing tells us something about the shock of the new. By the 1920s, Ferrucio Bonavia argued, such musical devices prompted little more than a flicker of a smile on the lips, but in 1896 they had represented a manifestation of 'a daring subject treated in daring fashion'.[32] This was an entirely new type of opera, for sure, but with reviews like this there was little to indicate that it was one that would gain any sort of long-term foothold in the repertory.

Comments about the opera's plot and music were not universally negative, and audiences and critics would, in due course, attune their ears to the novelties of Puccini's score. Puccini's supporters fought back against Wagnerian comparisons with the claim that the simplicity of La bohème was a virtue, and they revelled in what they heard as the work's abundantly rich melodic qualities and its sheer sensuality. This led to bold yet rather vague patriotic claims about its inherent 'Italianness', the Milanese newspaper La perseveranza indulging in a moment of musical flag-waving by declaring the opera to be a 'precious document that affirms that the ancient, glorious flag of our art still flies high'.[33]

POPULAR APPEAL

Another topic that drew a variety of opinions both negative and positive from critics in different countries was Puccini's wide appeal to ordinary people. Puccini was already gaining a reputation by this time as the musical voice of the growing Italian middle classes. On the face of it this should have been unproblematic in the Italian context, where opera played to audiences across the class spectrum and occupied a position not far removed from the world of contemporary popular culture. Indeed, one might say that it received the ultimate accolade of success in spawning popular parodies, such as *Na Bohêma*, performed in Naples in Neapolitan dialect in May 1896.[34] Nevertheless, later in Puccini's lifetime, from around 1910 onwards, a fringe group of intellectual commentators would cast writing for the bourgeoisie as something rather contemptible, as we shall see in the next chapter.

But after a slightly shaky start, audiences in Italy fell in love with the opera, as they did even more quickly in cities around the world. In Mexico City in August 1897, for example, a critic for *La Voz de México* reported:

> There is no record of a more complete triumph in the performances of the current Italian opera company than that obtained by the première of Puccini's work on Saturday night. The young Italian composer who received ovations in all the major European theatres, has now also conquered the Mexican public. At the beginning the audience was quite reserved, but by the end of the first act it was won over and applauded the work and the artists with enthusiasm.[35]

In some national contexts, as here, popular success was an indicator of success *tout court*. In others, it was a problem. Some Austrian critics, for example, were condescending about what they saw as the opera's embarrassingly middle-brow qualities from the start. A reviewer for the *Wiener Tagblatt* accused Puccini of creating, in Rodolfo and Mimì's separation scene, 'A bad *coup de théâtre*, a dubious concession to the sentimentality of a bourgeois public, a moral bottle of smelling salts'.[36] There is more than a whiff of distaste at Puccini's popularity here, a charge of kitsch. This too would become a recurring refrain in the work's transnational reception over the decades to follow.

In America the opera prompted a slightly different sort of squeamishness: a certain moral outrage. Here the opera's problem was not that it was too sentimental but too seedy. An unnamed critic for *The New York Times*, for example, protested in 1900 at the low morals exhibited in *La bohème* and argued that 'the celebration of the scarlet woman seems to be almost unavoidable in the drama of today'. The author declared himself depressed that 'the glorification of the imperfect woman' should be considered a suitable subject for operatic treatment at all, and announced that 'Mimi is a drab, and all the tears wasted over her unfortunate fate are wasted'.[37] (The noun 'drab' was used at this time to mean a slattern or prostitute.)

It is intriguing that Mimì—so much toned down from Murger's version and often seen now as a rather angelic figure—should have prompted comment along these lines. American critics argued about whether *La bohème* or *La traviata* was more offensive in its subject matter. Krehbiel found Puccini's opera by far the worse, arguing that:

> *La bohème* is foul in subject and fulminant, but futile, in its music. Its heroine is a twin sister of the woman of the camellias, whose melodious death puts such a delightfully soothing balm upon our senses that we forget to weep in Verdi's opera. But Mimi is fouler than Camille, alias Violetta, and Puccini has not been able to administer the palliative which lies in Verdi's music.[38]

This sort of attitude is less discernible in European responses to the opera. Mahler noted that the subject matter might have had the potential to shock but that the propriety of the language used in the libretto, and the charming music, had avoided any such perils. Parts of Leoncavallo's *Bohème*, on the other hand, he deemed 'lewd'.[39]

In terms of popular appeal, a noteworthy strand that emerges from the early British reviews is the way in which the opera was constructed as resolutely non-highbrow from the start. For the first performance at Covent Garden by the Carl Rosa Company, the opera was billed explicitly as 'popular opera' intended for a mixed audience. The pricing was altered 'for a cheap season' and so too was the layout of the auditorium: rows of seats were removed from the stalls in order to form a spacious pit and private boxes were removed and replaced by first, second, and third circles. *The St James' Gazette* reported that 'The convenience, in fact, of that important body "the general public" has been studied in every way'.[40]

For some of the critics, however, the suspicion that Puccini had consciously written the opera for a popular audience was not a matter for celebration. The critic for *The Pall Mall Gazette* wrote that 'It cannot be denied . . . that he gives one the impression upon many occasions of deliberately writing down to the level of a popular audience'.[41] This critic's particular complaint revolved around the stylistic echoes he perceived here and there (such as in the Mimì–Rodolfo duet) of the modern drawing-room ballad, which he called 'that peculiar compound of musical sentimentalism, obviousness, prettiness and vulgarity . . . a thing to be held in everlasting abhorrence by any man of taste'. In Puccini's hands this was, without doubt, ballad writing of the highest order, but it was ballad writing nevertheless and had prompted in the composer 'a terrible temptation to desert his better self'.

A comment from *The Illustrated Sporting and Dramatic News* is also particularly telling: 'the music . . . has a facile charm that makes it agreeable enough to listen to, but not to recall with any degree of intellectual satisfaction. *La bohème* is captivating in its way, and its melodic beauty is beyond question, and viewed from any standpoint lower than that of grand opera, its merit would be freely and gratefully acknowledged'.[42] The way in which Puccini appeared to be attempting to straddle the art–entertainment divide—enjoyable enough but lacking serious or transcendental qualities—would be problematic for him throughout his entire career.

LOCALISED CONCERNS

Some of the other strands that emerged from the early international reception of *La bohème* were particular to their local performance context. The French response is worthy of note, of course, because of the Parisian setting of the piece. The work was a huge popular triumph at its première at the Opéra-Comique in 1898. Critical responses included some dissenting voices but were largely positive: the critic for *Le XIX siècle* summed it up by noting that the opera pleased the eyes, the ears, and the heart, made one laugh and made one cry, and asking what more one could want?[43] Unlike some other national premières of the opera, the French one, which was supervised by Puccini, was felt to have done the work justice. Critics were almost entirely united in praising the cast, led by Adolphe

Maréchal, a Belgian tenor who had arrived at the Opéra-Comique three years previously and who would later create the leads in *Louise* and several Massenet works, and the soprano Julia Guiraudon, a house regular, who was deemed by Pougin to be 'a truly exquisite Mimì'.[44] (Her costume is shown in figure 3.2.)

As one might expect, the French reception was particularly attentive to the opera's relationship to its preceding literary sources. Although Puccini and his librettists had drawn primarily upon Murger's novel, French reviewers drew comparisons with Barrière's drama, which was running at the Comédie-Française in parallel with Puccini's opera: play and opera were reviewed side by side in several publications, and publicity for one generated publicity for the other.[45] (Amusingly, *Le Gaulois* reported confusion on the part of users of the théâtrophone—a system which allowed subscribers to listen to a theatrical performance over the telephone lines—who were given access to Barrière's play when they wanted Puccini's opera, and vice versa, since both were entitled *Vie de Bohème*.[46]) Some critics complained that the librettists had captured little of the spirit of the original, focusing upon the central romance to the exclusion of all else: one argued that the opera should have been entitled *Rodolphe et Mimi*.[47] However, others recognised that the librettists were simply following the conventions imposed upon them by the Italian operatic genre, in extracting the essential elements and rejecting everything that would hold up the action.[48]

In Britain, meanwhile, there was no such framework of familiar reference, but the press used other strategies to 'domesticate' the piece. Many critics treated *La bohème* as if it were

FIGURE 3.2   Costume for the character of Mimì from *La bohème* by Giacomo
Puccini, sketch by Marcel Multzer (1866–1937), 1898, Opéra
Comique theatre in Paris, nineteenth century / Bibliothèque de
l'Opéra Garnier, Paris, France / De Agostini Picture Library /
Bridgeman Images.

an *English* opera first and foremost, no doubt in part because of hearing it for the first time in the vernacular. (Amusingly, reviewers made condescending complaints about the English pronunciation of the two Italian leading men who joined the cast for the London première, Messrs Salvi and Maggi.[49]) Critics sought to contextualise the opera for audiences by using home-grown artworks and even contemporary celebrities as points of reference. *The Liverpool Mercury*, for instance, noted the resemblance between Marcello and 'our own Clive Newcome', a contemporary British watercolour painter.[50]

Most striking among the familiarising strategies was the way in which numerous critics compared the opera's subject to that of George Du Maurier's *Trilby* as a way of selling Puccini's work to audiences.[51] Du Maurier's novel was in itself an intertextual response to Murger's scenes of Bohemian life, and an important vehicle for creating stereotypes about Parisian low life for a British readership. Like the Murger, it was also a highly rambling, episodic text, in which atmosphere was arguably more important than narrative. *Trilby* had been the literary sensation of 1894, a best-seller about aspiring (British) artists in the Latin Quarter of Paris that in turn prompted an array of spin-offs in the form of songs, literary parodies, and stage adaptations.[52] It is interesting to see *La bohème* being associated with *Trilby* fever, particularly as Du Maurier's unchaste heroine prompted moral panic among the guardians of Victorian virtue. Both works undoubtedly played into an Anglo-Saxon curiosity about the phenomenon of Bohemia—then a rather exotic concept within the British context.[53]

In the United States, meanwhile, the early *La bohème* reviews reveal an interesting strand in historical performance practice. The opera was initially performed in conjunction with other works, or parts of other works: on tour in Los Angeles, Denver, Kansas City, and Minneapolis, performances by the Metropolitan Opera Company concluded with Melba singing the mad scene from *Lucia di Lammermoor*. Such an eclectic pairing would strike us nowadays as frankly bizarre, and one might question the need to supplement a full-length opera with an additional operatic scene full-stop. But *La bohème* was, of course, not yet tried-and-tested in 1900, and Puccini's music more generally was comparatively little known, so adding a guaranteed crowd-pleaser by a popular star of the day was a useful, perhaps even necessary, tactic to draw in an audience.

Furthermore, it was routine practice at the Met in the late nineteenth century and the first few decades of the twentieth to package two or more operas, or scenes from operas, into a single evening's entertainment. New York had a reputation as the capital of the operatic star system and audiences were interested first and foremost in listening to famous singers performing 'the good bits' from well-known operas; within such a culture, dramatic integrity was a low priority. Unusual performances of *La bohème* would continue for some years. In February 1906, for example, it was staged with the peculiar interpolation between Acts 2 and 3 of a short one-act play, in which the star bass Pol Plançon (who did not appear in Puccini's opera itself), sang the *Marseillaise*.[54] The association of *La bohème* with celebrity figures is something I shall address in greater detail in the next chapter.

Within only a few years of its première, then, *La bohème* appeared to have established itself in the international operatic repertory, although it was still by no means as central to it as it is today. The opera was one that popped up from time to time at any given theatre but not as an annual event. At the Teatro Regio in Turin, for instance, the opera was not performed between 1898 and 1908, nor between 1916 and 1927, and it was a similar story at La Scala, with no performances between 1901 and 1916.[55] The opera caught on more quickly and was performed with far greater regularity in southern Italy.

As a decade and more passed after the première, Puccini's biographers began to reflect retrospectively upon the work's rise to prominence. In some cases these accounts mythologised the opera's early reception and are not always trustworthy. A tendency to gloss over inconvenient facts is revealed in Wakeling Dry's patently incorrect assertion of 1906 that the opera 'captured the Italian ear and taste immediately'.[56] (One *hopes*, however, that there is truth in his claim that in Italy the work produced a generation of baby Mimìs and Rodolfos.)

The flawed simplicity of such an account as Dry's is revealed if we compare it with that of Vincent Seligman, writing with greater critical distance in 1938 and drawing upon correspondence exchanged between his mother Sybil and Puccini himself. He noted that in Turin the reception was 'little more than cordial', the Press 'almost unanimously hostile' and that 'what really does appear surprising in retrospect is the extreme slowness with which the public themselves grew aware of the merits of the new opera'.[57] Seligman observed that the opera's focus on everyday life, its high spirits and mixture of laughter and tears should in theory have made it an instant success, 'and yet the very reverse was the case'.[58] In spite of its early troubles, the opera had, Seligman argued, proved itself to be both time-proof and fool-proof, being performed more often than any opera other than *Madama Butterfly* and withstanding the indignity of being performed by 'screeching Musettas', 'grandmotherly Mimìs', and 'heavy-weight Rodolfos'.[59]

For all of the negativity that initially surrounded the work—more to do with the critics' struggles to position it within the contemporary operatic landscape than the opera itself—*La bohème* slowly but surely secured its place in the performing repertory of most of the leading opera houses of the Western hemisphere. Its sheer popularity with audiences meant that it was a work that opera house managers could not resist. Furthermore, as Puccini's compositional style began to become more adventurous—starting with *La fanciulla del West* in 1910 and continuing with *Il tabarro* (1917) and *Turandot* (1926)—*La bohème* seemed increasingly comforting in comparison, with its lyricism (now far more apparent than it was on a first hearing), its relative lack of musical complexity, and its gentle romance.

From the turn of the 1920s, critics and biographers would start to speak about Puccini's oeuvre being divided into two distinct 'manners', the more conservative first manner being constructed as 'sincere', the second more experimental one as something Puccini surely couldn't have truly meant. But *La bohème* was prized even more highly than some of his other 'first manner' works, particularly *Tosca*. 'Intellectual' music was still actively disparaged by the majority of Italian critics at this point. For instance, Adriano Lualdi, a composer, conductor, and by the time of writing a Mussolini acolyte, was typical in lauding *La bohème* in 1928 for being 'a work of theatre and not a university thesis'.[60] By the 1920s, then, *La bohème* had become not only a work concerned with nostalgia as a dramatic theme but one that seemed to embody nostalgia itself, for a golden age both in Puccini's career and in the history of Italian opera.

CHAPTER 4

POPULARISING LA BOHÈME

What manner of man is this whose operas are played upon the stages of all the opera-houses; whose choicest melodies, wrenched from their environment with a supreme disregard for the niceties of taste, are pressed into service to provide a harmonious background for the clatter of knives and forks in numerous restaurants and compelled to pay their tribute to modern conditions by being recorded on the gramophone; to whose airs foreign barons sip their after-dinner coffee in international hotels?[1]

T HESE WORDS, WRITTEN IN 1917 by the critic D. C. Parker in *The Musical Quarterly*, sum up the position in which Puccini found himself by the 1910s. Italian opera had never, of course, been strictly confined to its own particular environment, much to the consternation of self-styled highbrow commentators. During the late nineteenth century, for example, its melodies had been routinely appropriated by street musicians, brass band players, and

Puccini's La bohème. Alexandra Wilson, Oxford University Press (2021). © Oxford University Press.
DOI: 10.1093/oso/9780190637880.001.0001.

music hall performers. But Puccini's music seemed to lend itself to an altogether more audacious degree of boundary crossing. As Parker surmised, his melodies had become veritable commodities, perfectly adapted to the world of modern recording and equally well suited to being exploited as background music in the lively and glamorous new entertainment industry of the early twentieth century.

Was the fact that Puccini's music could function in this way a problem, or something to be celebrated? For his own part, Parker—a Puccini enthusiast by and large, albeit immune to the charms of *La fanciulla del West*—seemed comparatively unconcerned. However, his reference to 'the niceties of taste' nods to a wider critical disapproval, and the question 'what kind of man is this' hints at some sort of character flaw on Puccini's part. Many other commentators of the day, and indeed of subsequent decades, would take a far less forgiving view: Puccini's oeuvre did, indeed, raise questions about good and bad taste, as well as about other troubling matters concerning modernity, artistic integrity, and commercialism. Put simplistically, some modernist critics' assessment of good art during this period hinged to a large extent upon a scrupulous denial of pleasure, a measure by which Puccini's works were doomed to fail. While the previous chapter documented initial responses to *La bohème*, this one examines how responses to Puccini developed across the course of the twentieth century, with a particular focus upon the composer's 'problematic' popularity and the relationship of his opera to the wider entertainment industry.

La bohème may have secured a position within the international performing repertory by the 1900s, but Puccini had by no means yet garnered critical respect for his compositional style and here there is a much more complex story to be told. We need to step away from our specific opera briefly in order to understand the wider debates that circled around the composer's works in the early twentieth century. During Puccini's lifetime his works attracted sharply polarised responses from Italian critics, ranging from the hagiographic at one extreme to the excoriating at the other. These debates went far beyond purely musical matters, as both Puccini the man and his works became caught up in broader discussions about how to form an Italian cultural identity in the aftermath of political Unification (a decades-long process completed by 1870). Italy might have been firmly established as a single nation by the 1890s—the peninsula had previously consisted of a collection of independent states—but there was still only a vague sense of what it meant to be Italian, as regional allegiances remained strong and many citizens continued to speak local dialects and lacked common experiences. The artistic establishment of the day identified opera as a valuable tool that could be used to give the new Italians a shared cultural reference point. However, Puccini's works did not always fulfil the nationalist hopes invested in them, as I have discussed in more detail elsewhere.[2]

There were many reasons—some political, some artistic, some more personal—why Puccini caused offence to the sterner musical commentators of the day, but central among the objections was the perception that his works were too commercial: his financial success was, by definition, a black mark against him. As D. C. Parker observed at the time, 'Conventions die hard and there is a lingering romantic notion that the real poet is to be found only in the gutter, the real musician only in the attic. When, therefore, fate plays us a strange trick and we discover the former in easy circumstances and the latter with a good dinner to eat the serious person becomes suspicious'.[3] In other words, people continued to expect Puccini to live like one of his own Bohemians if he were to maintain critical respect: a Romantic mythology that his patrons built around him and to which he had himself contributed would ultimately come back to bite him.

Highbrow critics attacked Puccini in his own time and for decades after for being overly sentimental and manipulative, for revealing the seams of his operas a little too obviously. However, more sympathetic commentators have observed that it was precisely this mastery of theatrical effect that made Puccini's works so successful: he knew what he wanted to do, and he was capable of doing it with aplomb. The conductor Thomas Beecham, for example, detected in Puccini 'a highly developed inner visual sense . . . that sees as in an ever-present mirror the progress of the drama running through every phrase, word, and action, and simultaneously evolves the right sort of music to go along with it'.[4]

As time went on, critics increasingly labelled Puccini as a composer who 'knew his limitations', observing that he was working within a restricted artistic and intellectual orbit.[5] In the hands of most critics, this was intended as disparagement, a consigning of Puccini to the second rank of composers. Occasionally, however, it comes over more positively, as for example in the words, once again, of D. C. Parker: 'He writes with a gusto and zest, and with him there is no equivalent of the problems which confront us when we approach Wagner, Bruneau, Scriabin and others. No propaganda, no philosophy, is forced down your throat. By his own confession he is determined not to trespass beyond the point at which he feels at home'.[6] The point that Parker puts his finger on here is not so much that Puccini had limited horizons but that he gave himself completely unto theatrical pleasure and that perhaps we ought to yield to it as well.

But Puccini was undoubtedly the victim of a broader snobbery about Italian opera per se: a perception that it was a vehicle for the indulgence of stupid singers and a form of frivolous distraction for even more stupid audiences. Of course, many of the aspects of Italian opera that were regarded as particularly egregious—endless virtuosic arias with clear applause points and a lack of concern for dramatic realism—no longer really applied to a work such as *La bohème*. Nevertheless, early twentieth-century commentators of a modernist viewpoint often condemned all composers of post-Rossinian Italian opera in one fell swoop. Take, for instance, the comments of the French music critic Georges Jean-Aubry, writing in a British periodical in 1920:

> One is easily disposed to think that one has done justice to Italy after having made the acquaintance of a few operas by Verdi, Puccini, Leoncavallo and Mascagni, although it must be stated at once that these represent only the most mediocre and perishable part of Italian musical expression. Granted that such works have proved long and profitable successes, that famous tenors continue to use them as a foil to their triumphs; granted that in certain towns the glory of Verdi equals that of Wagner; but to judge musical Italy exclusively by its operatic creations of the

second half of the 19th century, would be equivalent to judging French literature of the last century by the novels of François Coppée, English literature by Mrs Humphrey Ward, or Russian music by the one and only Tchaikovsky.[7]

Puccini's works, according to this and similar accounts of the period, were cheap and disposable. The comparisons that Jean-Aubry draws are worth noting. Tchaikovsky, of course, needs no introduction, but was regarded during this period and later by serious music critics as more of a craftsman than a serious artist. The French novelist and poet Coppée, meanwhile, was known as 'le poète des humbles', which brings to mind Puccini's famous preoccupation with life's 'little things'. And Mrs Humphrey Ward (Mary Augusta Ward) was an author who wrote best-selling novels, magazine stories, and children's literature. Such comparisons were not flattering to a composer who was supposedly the flag-bearer for contemporary Italian culture.

The broader gist of Jean-Aubry's initially dismissive article was that there was good Italian music to be found, if one were prepared to look beyond the opera house and music that he regarded as tasteless tourist-fodder. He expressed enthusiasm for early music (Monteverdi, Caldara, Scarlatti, Pergolesi) and advocated the case of contemporary non-operatic composers including Pizzetti, Casella, Malipiero, and the Futurists. Here his enthusiasms and antipathies—anything but nineteenth-century opera, in essence—are conspicuously similar to those of Fausto Torrefranca, a notorious figure in Puccini reception studies, who emblematises the way in which daggers would really start to be drawn against the composer in the second decade of the twentieth century. In a remarkable intertwining of music and politics, Torrefranca blamed Italian opera—and Puccini's in particular—for all of the recently united nation's ills.

Torrefranca, a twenty-nine-year-old critic and aspiring musicologist, published a polemical book in 1912 entitled *Giacomo Puccini e l'opera internazionale*, which attacked Puccini's music, his approach to drama, and above all his persona.[8] The book was both a scathing character assassination and a piece of aesthetic snobbery of the first order: Torrefranca mocked Puccini for being too populist and his middle-class audience for being 'culturally semi-illiterate'. His book probably had little more than a modest dissemination, limited primarily to north-Italian intellectual circles. Nevertheless, it undoubtedly had a disorientating effect upon the thin-skinned Puccini himself and informed the writings of later critics.

The essence of Torrefranca's argument was that Puccini's operas—and indeed operas in general—were symptomatic of a 'decadence' currently afflicting Italian culture, leading it to become conservative, bourgeois, and effeminate. (We should bear in mind that Torrefranca, despite being a bookish intellectual, vigorously endorsed a movement on the political far right that advocated a new brand of violent, hyper-macho nationalism.) Puccini's male characters (figure 4.1), Torrefranca argued, were reflections of a broader softening of the national character and as weak and feeble as their creator. *La bohème*'s Rodolfo and Marcello were, like their predecessor Des Grieux and successor Pinkerton, 'invertebrate men': spineless, sickly, neurotic, and unmanly. Mimì, meanwhile, was an emblem of Puccini himself, whom Torrefranca depicts as 'the perfect womanly

FIGURE 4.1   Postcard by Adolfo Hohenstein (1854–1928) created on the
occasion of the première of *La bohème* by Giacomo Puccini
(1858–1924), depicting a scene from Act 4 / De Agostini Picture
Library / A. Dagli Orti / Bridgeman Images.

musician' and indeed a lower-class woman, specifically a
seamstress.[9]

Eight years later, Jean-Aubry—apparently echoing
Torrefranca in tone and terms of reference, although we
cannot know for sure that he read his book—argued that
Italian tastes were starting to shift away from the ubi-
quitous opera in favour of more avant-garde music.[10] He
argued that:

> The twilight of the 'verists' has set in and their disappear-
> ance is only a question of time. Although *La bohème*,
> *Cavalleria rusticana* and *Tosca* are still favourites, it is al-
> ready the singers that appear in them rather than the works

which are the main interest. In ten years nothing will remain of these works but gramophone records and the exhalations of barrel-organs.[11]

Hindsight is a wonderful thing, and Jean-Aubry's was one of numerous gaffes critics made during Puccini's lifetime about the presumed unlikely longevity of his success. (See also Compton Mackenzie, editor of *Gramophone* magazine, who wrote in the 1930s that 'It is . . . improbable that a century hence anybody will be moved by *Traviata* or by *Bohème*'.[12]) But even though Jean-Aubry's prediction was incorrect, his argument about star singers and recordings and their role in popularising the opera is an interesting one, which can help us to understand *La bohème*'s supposedly 'problematic' relationship with broader popular culture and the role played by celebrity singers and recordings in cementing the popularity of the opera in the early twentieth century.

CELEBRITY

It is self-evident that *La bohème* is not a star vehicle in the manner of operas such as Bellini's *Norma*. The première in Turin used singers who could work together well on stage, rather than the biggest names of the day. In Puccini's mind, performers who could represent the roles credibly were essential: he praised the cast of the British première for its spontaneity and energy in spite of what was, by all accounts, a performance lacking in finesse.[13] Following this lead, Mamontov was careful to avoid celebrity casting for the Russian première, going so far as to pass over his company's star bass, Feodor Chaliapin, since to employ him would have given the role of Colline undue prominence, upsetting the dramaturgical balance of the piece as a whole.[14]

La bohème remains capable of attracting audiences on its own merits: not only is it an ensemble piece but opera companies still manage to sell it profitably with little-known or unknown casts. Indeed, the avoidance of starry casts may in some cases be not so much a budgetary necessity as a deliberate aesthetic choice. Consider, for instance, Baz Luhrmann's selection of a relatively little-known younger cast (headed by Cheryl Barker and David Hobson) in order to emphasise the opera's 'everyman' quality in his 1993 production for Opera Australia, which went on to attract international attention.

Nevertheless, as *La bohème* became more and more successful, it was inevitable that it would in due course become a vehicle for stars, who were ostensibly keen to depict Puccini's starving students and yet sometimes not quite willing to assume the roles with complete credibility. Early in the opera's history, the role of Mimì became closely associated with one particular celebrated singer: Nellie Melba (figure 4.2). Melba had studied the opera with Puccini personally, spending six weeks with him in Lucca, during which he coached her, she claimed, in 'his personal impressions of how the opera should be sung'.[15] She would perform the role of Mimì to great acclaim in major cities around the world but became particularly associated with it at Covent Garden. She sang in the first Italian-language production of the opera at the theatre in 1899, and her performances there with Enrico Caruso in the early 1900s became the stuff of legend. Symbolically, *La bohème* was also the first opera in which Melba sang upon returning to Covent Garden after

FIGURE 4.2   Nellie Melba, 1905. J. Willis Sayre Collection of Theatrical
Photographs. University of Washington: Special Collections.
Wikimedia Commons. No permission needed.

World War I, and she chose to perform scenes from it in her farewell concert at the theatre in 1926.

The endorsement of the opera by the biggest female star of her day undoubtedly helped to cement the opera's popularity, but it was not necessarily a recommendation in the eyes of a musical establishment sceptical of the celebrity circus that they saw as surrounding Italian opera. The critic for *The New York Times* who was so scathing of the opera at the Met in 1900, for instance, argued that the audience was not interested in the opera's plot, caring only that Melba was singing a new role and that her Rodolfo, Albert Saléza, was convincing as an ardent lover. Each, then, was merely fulfilling their accustomed role within the contemporary operatic ecosystem: Melba as the big star who had to be watched whatever she appeared in, and Saléza as a noted heart-throb. Puccini's own role, meanwhile, was a purely servile one, since 'A composer is only a musical tailor who makes melodic garments for great performers'.[16]

Comments about Melba's deficiencies as an actress were also widespread, although her voice was generally perceived to compensate. The fact that dramatic integrity was a far lower priority than a beautiful voice needs to be placed within the context of an early twentieth-century operatic performing culture in which acting was, for the most part, unsophisticated, or even virtually non-existent. At Covent Garden in 1900, for example, the tenor Alessandro Bonci—Melba's regular Rodolfo in London before Caruso—indulged in old-fashioned practices: singing to the footlights and performing encores that interfered with the flow of the dramatic narrative.[17]

When a star singer appeared in an opera, it was often perceived that they were 'playing themselves' rather than the character in question. That Melba did not really look the part as Mimì was frequently noted, but such concerns were typically put to one side as irrelevant. A critic for *The County Gentleman* wrote in praise of her voice and argued: 'The fact that physically the prima donna was quite unsuited to the part is a trifling matter, for none would be glad to see her as the thin consumptive woman Murger described in his gloomy romance'.[18] The idea that audiences—at least in some national contexts—would not *want* to see a realistic Mimì is telling, reinforcing the idea that *La bohème* was expected to represent poverty only at a certain remove.

Then there was the question of age. In 1899, Melba was already, at thirty-eight, on the older side of credibility for the role of Mimì, who must surely be meant to be barely out of her teens. But what is truly astonishing is that she was still playing her in the early 1920s, by which time she was in her sixties. Melba, then, undoubtedly pushed the suspension of disbelief to the limits. Nevertheless, in 1935 the venerable music critic Ernest Newman offered an interesting perspective on the question of dramatic plausibility, suggesting that the role of Puccini's heroine should *not* be offered to the young, lithe, and pretty singers one might ostensibly consider ideal for it. It was easy for such women to play Mimì and far more interesting to see a stout middle-aged woman attempt the part, 'for then, if she has any gift at all as an actress, I am interested in the spectacle of the constant conflict between her art and her handicap, and am the more ready to give her credit when the former is triumphant'.[19]

Melba was not, of course, the only singer whose performances in *La bohème* have stretched credibility. Think, for instance, of Pavarotti as a notably corpulent 'starving' student opposite Kiri Te Kanawa at Covent Garden, Mirella Freni at the San Francisco Opera, or Renata Scotto at the Met. But once again, the beautiful voice prompted forgiveness for a lack of dramatic plausibility, or at least indulgence. J. B. Steane writes of Pavarotti: 'He has never, I dare say, been much of an actor, yet several of his characters (think of the *Bohème* Rodolfo, for instance) remain vivid as genuine creations'.[20] And if one might have reservations about Pavarotti's interpretation of the role on stage, one could scarcely quibble with it on disc.

RECORDINGS AND REWORKINGS

Let us return now to Jean-Aubry's prediction that by the 1930s *La bohème* and other Puccini works would live on only via gramophone records. This was patently not to be the case, but recordings certainly served as helpful advertisements for the operas themselves, boosting their popularity in live performance. There have been countless complete recordings of *La bohème*, with a particular abundance of now-classic studio recordings being released around the middle of the twentieth century, with legendary Mimìs and Rodolfos including Victoria De Los Angeles and Jussi Björling (Beecham, 1956) and Freni and Pavarotti (Karajan, 1972).[21] Such big-budget landmark recordings were undoubtedly a factor in *La bohème*'s canonisation over the course of the twentieth century, as in due course were video recordings of emblematic casts. (A quick Amazon search for *La bohème* DVDs brings up almost as many 'vintage' casts from the 1960s to the 1980s as present-day ones.) In the days of the gramophone, however, it was excerpts that held sway, owing in part to practical considerations—the short time allowable on each record side—and in part to the popularity of individual arias in stand-alone context on the concert platform.

Opera loomed large in the early recording catalogue. In 1920s Britain *Strand* magazine reported *La bohème* to be vying for the top spot in public popularity with—of all things—excerpts from Wagner's *Ring*.[22] Puccini's opera was so fashionable, the magazine's correspondent claimed, because it was a favourite of the King and Queen. Some commentators of this period argued that there was already a surfeit of recordings of excerpts from the opera: a reviewer for *Gramophone* in 1927 welcomed a selection from Tchaikovsky's *Pique Dame* as 'a relief from perpetual *Bohème*s and *Madame Butterflies*'.[23]

The specific numbers recorded regularly will come as no surprise: Rodolfo's and Mimì's arias, the love duet, and Musetta's waltz song, plus occasionally 'O Mimì, tu più non torni' and 'Vecchia zimarra'. 'Che gelida manina' was recorded particularly frequently. As early as 1923, *Gramophone* reported that 'Almost every tenor sings this number and most collectors of records will possess one version or another of it'.[24] The magazine published an introductory guide to the aria the following year, providing readers with a translation of the text and a summary of where it fitted into the opera dramatically, and listing some twenty-seven tenors who had recorded it variously in Italian, English, French, and German.[25] It was common practice at this time for listeners to purchase a particular aria in multiple different renditions, and attendees of the many British 'gramophone clubs' would listen to different recordings and discuss their merits.

As one of the most popular opera composers of the early twentieth century, it is unsurprising that Puccini should also have lured early film directors. The concept of a silent film of an opera (or scenes from it) might seem like an oxymoron, but early film drew extensively on opera for inspiration, borrowing its popular and well-known plots and its melodramatic stage gestures. Furthermore, silent films were not, of course, really silent: live accompaniment was provided in the cinema by a musician, or an ensemble of musicians, which might include singers, and operatic arias were also frequently performed during live prologues that preceded the film proper.[26] At least eight silent films were adapted from *La bohème* during the 1910s and 1920s and numerous early talkies were loosely based upon it. Some (for reasons of copyright) claimed that they were based on Murger's version rather than the opera, but Puccini's music was played and sung during screenings.[27]

Within the two-year period 1910–11 alone, for instance, three short *La bohème* films appeared—each in a condensed format lasting no more than fifteen minutes—one American (from the Edison Studio), one French (Pathé), and one Italian (Cines).[28] Longer filmic treatments of the subject followed in the later 1910s, including a seventy-minute Cosmopoli studio film in 1917 directed by Amleto Palermi, while Metro-Goldwyn-Mayer released a ninety-five-minute version in 1926, directed by King Vidor and starring Lillian Gish and John Gilbert. Puccini's opera was the point of departure, but the films often elaborated upon Giacosa and Illica's plot in various ways. In Vidor's version, for example, there is an extended subplot in which Mimi is pursued by a rich admirer and were it not for her death the film would end on a high, Rodolphe having written a hit play.

In the case of both the Cosmopoli and the MGM films, Ricordi refused permission for Puccini's music to be performed alongside screenings, although it was not always possible for this to be policed in practice. Such controlling tendencies belie a nervousness from both composer and publisher about control of the opera slipping out of their grasp. (In 1923, similarly, Puccini sought damages for plagiarism after learning that melodies from his works were being reworked as foxtrots in the United States.[29])

Any antipathy towards film on Puccini's part seems unexpected, given the close connections that have been drawn between his oeuvre and the cinematic genre: his operas are often regarded as anticipating techniques that would be employed in film at both the musical and dramatic level. But Puccini no doubt knew that too close an association with the form of entertainment that was perceived to be threatening opera's supremacy was something that would be held against him. The German musicologist Richard Specht, writing later in the 1930s, argued that Puccini's works were 'film drama in its frankest and most uncompromising form', 'poster art of the most blatant description, but painted with the most delicate water-colour technique, and often with genuine heart's blood'.[30] They were, to this mindset, simultaneously alluring and crude.

Later film music composers would also borrow much from Puccini's compositional style, full-scale filmed versions of his works would appear in cinemas and on video, and excerpts from his operas would be used at pivotal moments in films. (These include Sally Potter's *Thriller*, *Maggio musicale*, *Awakenings*, *Heavenly Creatures*, and *Italian for Beginners*.) Where music from *La bohème* is used in comparatively recent films, the choice of source opera tends to be more than incidental: some sort of intertextual connection is usually drawn between the plots of opera and film. Two memorable films in particular—Norman Jewison's *Moonstruck* (1987) and Joe Wright's *Atonement* (2007)— seem to engage in active dialogue with the work. Both reference *La bohème* in order to meditate upon the ways in which visual media engage with the topics of romance and desire.

Moonstruck is a romantic comedy set in Brooklyn Heights, which tells the story of a young widow who falls in love with her fiancé's estranged brother, who has lost a hand in a baking accident. *La bohème* is not only used in *Moonstruck*'s soundtrack, alongside classic love songs such as Dean Martin's 'That's amore', but looms large in its plotline: Ronny, the work's hero (Nicolas Cage), plays Puccini's opera repeatedly on record, and woos the heroine, Loretta (Cher), at a performance of the work at the Metropolitan Opera. *La bohème* becomes key to identity formation here, acting as a conscious diegetic soundtrack to the blossoming romance between these two quirky, flawed filmic protagonists, who identify with Puccini's characters and become transformed in the process. It is refreshing that Jewison shies away from the standard way of representing opera in film—as a signifier for luxury or high social status—and, rather, presents it as genuinely belonging to these decidedly unpretentious members of New York's Italian-American community. It is doubly refreshing, as Marcia J. Citron observes, that he allows both male and female protagonists to revel in the sheer, unabashed pleasure that the opera gives and in its heartfelt (or, to the cynic, clichéd) signifiers of romance.[31]

In *Atonement*—a tragic 1930s–1940s period drama based on the novel by Ian McEwan—*La bohème* is not consistently woven into the fabric in the same way that it is in *Moonstruck*, but Rodolfo's aria is used prominently in 'set piece' fashion in one particularly important scene.[32] The film's hero Robbie (James McAvoy) plays 'O soave fanciulla' on a record (just as Ronny does in *Moonstruck*), this time while writing a letter to the heroine, Cecilia (Keira Knightley). It is a letter that is highly passionate—indeed that verges on the indecent—and one that he does not intend actually to send. (The fact that it is delivered in error sets in motion a series of events that will have tragic consequences for both lovers.) The music helps Robbie to find the words he is struggling to express: opera, here, acts as muse.

Wright uses the act of listening to an opera recording as a crucial narrative device and once again, there is a suggestion that the character in the film identifies with the character in the opera. Robbie, like Ronny, appears to see himself as the romantic poet Rodolfo, professing his love to Cecilia, whom we see in a mirror preparing for the evening ahead whenever Mimì sings. The choice of a Puccini love duet alters the tone of the letter-writing scene considerably from the more buttoned-up way it is presented in Ian McEwan's original novel: with such an accompaniment, Robbie's emerging feelings are voiced passionately and unmistakably. As in *Moonstruck*, the sensual qualities of Puccini's music are, here, wholeheartedly embraced. In both films it is used as a vehicle of emerging, sensitive male love, and something that can speak to and for characters from across the class spectrum. Recent films, then, have not merely appropriated Puccini's music in clichéd fashion as signifiers of operatic excess or of Italianness. Rather—and more interestingly—they have engaged with *La bohème* in a very direct way, celebrating the opera and the ways in which it speaks to us, moves us, and allows us to explore our own romantic fantasies.

But sometimes Puccini's music has been used in popular culture as a signifier for a type of romance that seems clichéd, even perhaps tacky. Take, for example, an episode of the American TV series *Buffy the Vampire Slayer*, in which one of the lead characters, Rupert Giles, arrives home to find roses, champagne, a seductive note saying 'Upstairs', and 'O soave fanciulla' playing from an unseen stereo system. The mood is one of overt romantic and sexual anticipation (though it is blindingly obvious that upon going upstairs the character will discover his girlfriend dead in bed).[33] This use of Puccini's music—as a signifier of cheesy romance—chimes with a pronounced strand of embarrassment that has run through the Puccini reception from his own time to the present day, constructing his works as a guilty pleasure, something one could scarcely admit in polite company to liking. Caryl Flinn, for example, wrote in 2001 that 'tasteful people don't buy into, or rather, publicly admit buying into, the hamfisted pining of Rudolfo [*sic*] for Mimi'.[34]

The squeamishness surrounding the opera—the idea that it is too popular to count as good art—has been compounded by the fact that its arias, extracted from the opera per se, lie within the technical grasp of a range of different types of singers. At one end of the spectrum we might point to classically trained singers who crossed over successfully into the world of popular culture and celebrity, from Mario Lanza in the 1940s and 1950s to Pavarotti in the 1990s. At the other, Michael Bolton, purveyor of 1980s pop-rock ballads such as 'How Can I Live Without You?', performed 'Che gelida manina' and 'O soave fanciulla' (with Renée Fleming) on his 1998 album 'My Secret Passion' and live in concert. Many crossover performers, such as Andrea Bocelli and Alfie Boe (who performed Rodolfo at English National Opera and on Broadway for Baz Luhrmann before abandoning an operatic career) sit somewhere in between. The aesthetic quality of performances by these very different tenors may have been variable, but the expansion in audience reach has been inestimable. It is always hard to know, however, how many people make the leap from hearing an individual aria to watching a complete opera.

Puccini's melodies have also been introduced to listeners who were perhaps oblivious to their original provenance. A good example is the Bobby Worth song 'Don't You Know?', a million-selling hit in 1959 for American gospel/jazz singer Della Reese and derived from 'Quando m'en vo'. The ballad was released on an album called 'The Classic Della', which also included tracks based on works by Tchaikovsky, Schubert, and Chopin, but many listeners would have encountered 'Don't You Know?' in isolation. In this reworking, the opening theme of Musetta's aria is followed closely, both in the vocal line and accompaniment, and repeated many times, albeit interspersed with new material. In one sense, an 'operatic' mood is subtly maintained, at least as mediated via Hollywood. (There are far more souped-up orchestral flourishes in the song than in the aria, giving the former a glittering, schmaltzy feel; repeated listening to the two almost makes the operatic aria seem subdued.) But other aspects of the song are pure pop: the Frank-Sinatraesque big band arrangement; the well-worn convention of jacking up the key for emphatic effect towards the end; the reducing of the words to a simple confession of undying love ('Don't you know? I have fallen in love with you; for the rest of my whole life through').

'Don't You Know?' was then given even greater dissemination through cover versions by Susan Lane, Jerry Vale, Robie Porter, Jim Nabors, and the Lettermen, all recorded between 1959 and 1970 in an attempt to cash in on the success of the original hit. These versions moved steadily further and further away from 'Quando m'en vo' in stylistic arrangement and accompaniment, and were clearly, with one exception, using the Worth/Reese version as their starting point rather than going back to Puccini. (Vale's version—in proper crooner territory—reverts to the original by inserting as an introductory flourish the motif that is heard in the opera immediately before 'Quando m'en vo'.) The various covers are highly varied in style. Porter veers towards a country music ambience; Nabors's recording sounds like a cross between the Carpenters and a Disney soundtrack, with its shimmering chorus of cooing female voices. By the time we get to the version by the Lettermen, the song has been given a strange other-worldly gloss, with easy-listening strings, prominent drums, keyboard arpeggios, and high male voices in harmony. The influences here seem to have been the Righteous Brothers and the Beach Boys (with whom the Lettermen shared a record label) rather than Puccini. And yet something of the original melody remained, slowly but surely working its way into the public consciousness.

La bohème has also spawned larger-scale works of popular culture, which sit in intertextual relation to it. Some have been full-length theatrical works that used the opera as a point of inspiration, playing upon its popularity and reciprocally stimulating further interest in it. The 1937 Austrian musical film *Zauber der Boheme* (*The Charm of La bohème*, dir. Géza von Bolváry), in which Rodolfo and Mimì become René and Denise (played by Jan Kiepura and Mártha Eggerth), was loosely based on the plot of the opera, and incorporated sections of Puccini's score into an original soundtrack by the operetta composer Robert Stolz. Worlds away from this charming confection, and demonstrating the infinite adaptability of the *Bohème* storyline, director Mark Dornford-May relocated the story to contemporary tuberculosis-stricken South Africa in his 2015 film *Breathe Umphefumlo*. A condensed adaptation of Giacosa and Illica's libretto followed the exploits of a group of present-day students, while sections from Puccini's score were performed on marimbas and kettle drums and sung in the Xhosa language.[35] (Dornford-May had previously directed an adaptation of Puccini's opera with Isango Ensemble, featuring a cast of black singers from South African townships and steel-band accompaniment.[36])

There have also been theatrical works for which Murger's source text was technically the point of departure, but where composers and dramatists surely also capitalised upon the opera's contemporary success. Take, for example, the 1905 operetta *La Petite Bohème* by Henri Hirschmann (a former pupil of Massenet's) to a libretto by Paul Ferrier, which was staged at the Théâtre des Variétés in Paris in 1905. Certainly, the poster depicted Bohemians whose costumes—particularly the floppy ties of the men—and position around a table at the Café Momus were highly reminiscent of turn-of-the-century stagings of Puccini's opera. Hirschmann was at the very least clearly drawn to literary works that had already enjoyed success as operas: he would write a further work called *La Petite Manon* in 1913.

More familiar to most readers than any of these operettas or films will be two high-profile works that draw narrative inspiration from Puccini's opera. Jonathan Larson and Billy Aronson's successful 1990s Broadway musical *Rent* transfers a loose version of the *La bohème* story to New York's East Village, using a musical language influenced by rock, Motown, reggae, and the works of Stephen Sondheim (with a brief quotation from Musetta's waltz song).[37] In this reworking, HIV/AIDS is substituted for TB, and the Mimì character, an exotic dancer called Mimi Márquez, is not the only character to be afflicted.

A *Bohème* influence, albeit at one further remove, is also discernible in the film *Moulin Rouge!* (2001), directed by Baz Luhrmann, who had already had success with the aforementioned modern-dress production of Puccini's opera for Opera Australia, which subsequently transferred to Broadway. *Moulin Rouge!* does not borrow from *La bohème* musically: it is essentially a filmed musical, which works popular songs of its own period into its *fin-de-siècle* setting in quintessentially postmodern fashion. However, its plundering of elements of both *La traviata* and *La bohème* in terms of plot, setting, and characterisation is obvious. As Mina Yang observes, 'Luhrmann . . . fabricates a story about a pair of star-crossed lovers in *fin-de-siècle* Paris by rearranging and interpreting the archive of songs, plots and imageries contained in our collective memory'.[38] It is not inconceivable that the *Moulin Rouge!* representation of turn-of-the-century Paris in turn now feeds back into productions of *La bohème* to the extent that some audience members might consider the film the 'original' and the opera the response to it.

Throughout the twentieth century and beyond, then, Puccini has found himself at the centre of debates about where his works sat on the art-entertainment spectrum, and indeed about whether commercial success demeans the worth of a theatrical work. Today's professional music critics have by and large accepted that Puccini deserves his place in the operatic canon. On the other hand, academic snobbery about his works persists, even if his oeuvre has gained more credibility as the subject of scholarly investigation since the turn of the twenty-first century. However, academic agonising about Puccini's 'problematic' success is, of course, of little, or indeed no, concern to the average opera fan. Indeed, many audience members might be tempted to cheer at Parker's suggestion from 1917 that 'ultra-aesthetic' critics would be 'all the better for the good shaking up which the performance of a Puccini opera would give them'.[39] Nowadays, performances of Puccini's works, including *La bohème*, still 'shake up' viewers but in a way that would have been unimaginable to a commentator from 1917: through the ever-more unusual and varied ways in which they are interpreted and staged by contemporary directors. It is to this facet of *La bohème*'s story that we turn next.

CHAPTER 5

LA BOHÈME
REIMAGINED

M IMÌ WEARS A PUFFA jacket, beanie hat, and leopard-skin-print tight jeans; Schaunard the aspiring rock musician a leather biker's jacket daubed with graffiti. The Bohemians live in a cramped first-floor apartment in an anonymous brutalist block, Mimì two floors above them. We are not in the romanticised Paris of the *rive gauche* but an anonymous *cité HLM*: a high-rise estate of subsidised housing, typical of the sort built in the Parisian suburbs in the second half of the twentieth century, populated largely by immigrant communities. (Our Bohemians frequent the Caffè rather than the Café Momus.) Act 2 takes place at a flea market, where vendors have laid their goods out on blankets on the floor; a homeless person lies on a bench downstage throughout Act 3.

Puccini's La bohème. Alexandra Wilson, Oxford University Press (2021). © Oxford University Press.
DOI: 10.1093/oso/9780190637880.001.0001.

This is a production of *La bohème* directed by Àlex Ollé, one of the directors of the experimental Catalan theatrical group La Fura dels Baus, which was staged at the Teatro Regio in Turin in 2016 and transferred the following year to the Edinburgh International Festival. Many directors have updated Puccini's opera to more recent times, but in this case the gesture was especially striking, since the production was commissioned to commemorate the 120th anniversary of the opera's première at the same theatre. (In a new building: the Teatro Regio of Puccini's day was destroyed by fire in the 1930s.) One might have expected some deference to tradition in such a celebratory context, but Ollé's production was contemporary and resolutely unsentimental.

Such productions are not to all tastes. The approach taken by Ollé to Puccini's opera might seem surprising, even objectionable to some, yet I would argue that this is an effective and thought-provoking *Bohème*. Nothing in the libretto or action seems strained as a result of shifting the opera's time period, there is no gratuitous shock factor, and yet subtle details encourage the viewer to see the opera through new eyes. The costumes and sets reinforce the fact that most of the characters, barring certain patrons of the Momus, are working class; such nuances are less easy to grasp when long dresses, bonnets, and checked suits are the order of the day. Constructing an entire apartment block, of which the Bohemians occupy only a small part, gets around the problem of the garret the size of a ducal drawing room. And some critics have proposed that it is now hard to watch this production, in which the bare, grey metal skeleton of a tower block is exposed, without thinking of the shell of

West London's Grenfell Tower, and the fire in which many poor immigrants lost their lives in the summer of 2017.[1]

In this chapter, I examine the imaginative ways in which directors have updated *La bohème* in recent decades, either to the present day or to various other periods in living memory, by changing its sets, costumes, and occasionally fundamental aspects of its characterisation and dramaturgy (though never its music). The enduring success of some high-profile traditional productions is also considered. It is not my intention to write a blow-by-blow performance history of *La bohème*—the stagings have simply been too numerous—nor to identify a single 'ideal' presentation of the opera. But I use a selection of notable productions in order to trace changing directorial responses to the opera, which can, in turn, help us to understand what it has come to mean to audiences in recent times.

As a preamble, some historical context on operatic staging practices may be valuable. Transplanting operas to times more recent than those envisaged by their composers and librettists was a rare practice throughout the first three quarters of the twentieth century, let alone earlier. But operatic updating began to take off in earnest in the 1970s and has become almost *de rigueur* today, at least for certain works. In an era in which a comparatively small number of new operas are being written, opera as an art form functions predominantly as a form of museum culture, in which the same few core works are performed again and again. Thus, the only way to avoid endless similar productions is to stage such operas in new ways. Furthermore, in an era of limited arts funding, lavish, period-specific sets and costumes can be prohibitively expensive. But the motivations for operatic updating are not only pragmatic: many audience members and critics today welcome and expect directors to push at the boundaries of creativity.

On the other hand, operatic updating is greeted with nervousness in some quarters. This is more pronounced in the English-speaking world than, say, in Germany, where *Regietheater*—'director's theatre', based on the director's personal, often deliberately provocative, interpretation of the work—is the norm.[2] At the extreme conservative end of the spectrum, there are pockets of resistance to the idea of operatic updating per se (such as the creators and followers of the 'Against Modern Opera Productions' Facebook group). Such pressure groups tend to draw heavily upon the notion of 'the composer's intentions', insisting that these—or some vague assumption of what they might be—must be treated as sacrosanct. (This concept is intellectually flawed, not least because we do not always know whether the production that was staged initially was the composer's 'ideal' staging, or merely the best pragmatic possibility available to him or her at the time.) Equally, however, we might point to an occasional snobbery at the other end of the spectrum among some informed members of the opera audience towards any production that smacks of conservatism.

There can of course be good and bad updated productions of operas, just as there can be good and bad so-called traditional productions. It is certainly the case that some updated opera productions strain dramatic credibility to breaking point and that some directors adopt a deliberately sensationalist or self-indulgent approach. Furthermore, the argument that updating operas to the present is obligatory in order to make them 'relevant' or to bring in new audiences is facile, indeed perhaps even insulting to the intelligence of these imagined novice audience members, who presumably have no problem 'relating to' characters in films and television dramas set in Roman times or the Tudor period. However, operatic updatings are—when well conceived—undoubtedly a welcome and necessary means of giving vitality to the art form and encourage us to reconsider familiar works afresh.[3]

CONTINUITY AND LEGACY

Some of Puccini's operas might be considered somewhat stubbornly fixed in their original setting in terms of historical period and place. The specific set of geo-political circumstances that forms the backdrop for the *Madama Butterfly* story, for example, means that most directors continue to set the opera in Japan in the early twentieth century. Similarly, *La fanciulla del West* is another opera that directors rarely shift too far from its intended geographical setting—the American West—even if the sense of time is often hazy (jeans look plausible for any setting from the 1870s to the present).

In total contrast, *Gianni Schicchi* is an opera that is nowadays almost *never* set at its precisely defined historical moment: September 1, 1299. The current fashion is to move the action to the twentieth century, and most frequently to a stylised 1950s or 1960s, which plays into nostalgic, retro notions of 'Italianness' shaped by classic films.[4] The universality of the opera's dramatic theme (greedy relatives squabbling over a will) means that it can be relocated to almost any later period in history. The Florentine setting, however—thanks to Rinuccio's hymn of praise to the city and Lauretta's tongue-in-cheek threat to throw herself into the Arno—surely remains as unavoidable as a Californian one for *La fanciulla del West*. *Manon Lescaut*, meanwhile, is another opera that now tends to be routinely updated. This work was rather overlooked at the end of the twentieth century and the turn of the twenty-first, before exploding back on to the scene in recent years with high-profile productions at Covent Garden (directed by Jonathan Kent), the Met (Richard Eyre), and the Munich Opera (Hans Neuenfels). These productions reinvented the opera, casting aside its traditional, frilly, Rococo aesthetic and replacing it with sexy, glamorous settings that were either contemporary or influenced by a mid-twentieth-century film noir aesthetic.

La bohème falls somewhere between these two extremes: updating has not (yet) come to be seen as essential or compulsory but the opera lends itself easily to updating, should the director so choose. The opera is now regularly transplanted either to various emblematic periods of the twentieth century—Puccini's own time, the 1920s, the 1940s—or to the present. The iconography of Paris and the romantic symbolism surrounding the city have remained essential to many productions. Nevertheless, because Bohemia is—as we saw in chapter 2—something of a nebulous entity, directors have been more willing to transplant the action to other locations than they have in the case of works such as *Madama Butterfly*. Thus, for example, Stewart Laing relocated *La bohème* to the Williamsburg artistic community in contemporary Brooklyn for Scottish Opera in 2004 without any loss of dramatic effect, an airy loft standing in for the Parisian garret and the Museum of Modern Art replacing the Café Momus.[5]

The opera has, furthermore, been the object of a few very imaginative temporal *and* geographical relocations. In 2016, for instance, Opera Holland Park, in a positively received production by Stephen Barlow, took the most unusual step of projecting the action *backwards* in time to the theatrical milieu of Elizabethan London.[6] (Some critics discerned a nod to *Shakespeare in Love*, consistent with the fact that many opera directors now draw inspiration from films or other forms of popular culture with which audiences will be familiar.[7]) However, all such innovative productions—whether updated or, as critic and academic Mark Berry neatly describes the Barlow production, 'downdated'—coexist happily alongside numerous stagings of *La bohème* that continue to evoke a naturalistic early- or mid-nineteenth-century ambience and are not so very dissimilar from the way in which the opera was staged back in 1896.[8]

When considering the approaches that directors have taken to this opera, it is difficult to overlook a certain pragmatic consideration. For many opera companies, works such as *La bohème*, *La traviata*, and *Carmen* are obliged to operate as cash cows—safe works that demand relatively safe treatment in order to pull in the crowds and cross-subsidise more daring works. Some high-profile productions have proved themselves to be highly profitable across a period of many decades, particularly at theatres that need to meet the expectations of potentially conservative patrons and donors. At the time of writing, the Wiener Staatsoper is still using a Franco Zeffirelli production that has been staged annually since 1963: picturesque, faithful to the instructions in the libretto, and featuring in Act 2, as one critic put it, 'a cast of thousands, or at least hundreds, including a docile donkey which looked old enough to be an original cast member'.[9] La Scala is also still using a Zeffirelli production from the same year, which features similar long dresses, bonnets, and shawls, and a horse-drawn carriage in Act 2. The equally sumptuous Bayerische Staatsoper production by Otto Schenk dates from 1969.

Let us focus for a moment on two further scrupulously 'straight' productions that, perhaps not entirely by coincidence, were launched around the precise moment that operatic updating was starting to take off in earnest. These are John Copley's 1974 London production for the Royal Opera House, Covent Garden, and the 1981 production for the Metropolitan Opera in New York by—who else?—Franco Zeffirelli. Both productions consciously hark back to the aesthetic of the performances of Puccini's time, with a dash of late-twentieth-century ostentation thrown in. Indeed, so revered have these two productions been that one might argue that they have become canonical in their own right.

Zeffirelli's Met production is ultra-conservative and spares little expense, particularly in its staging of Act 2. It needed to work within the very particular operatic economy of the Met: the director had to create a production that was sufficiently sumptuous visually and risk-averse directorially as to fill a house with a capacity of almost 4,000 audience members and had to appeal to the tastes of wealthy patrons (see figure 5.1). But a predictable crowd-pleaser is not necessarily a critic-pleaser, and Zeffirelli's production has attracted attention for its bloated spectacle, amidst which it is easy for the characters in this most intimate of operas

FIGURE 5.1   *La bohème* from the Metropolitan Opera, April 2014, Bengt
Nyman. Licensed under the Creative Commons Attribution 2.0
Generic licence. Wikimedia Commons. No permission needed.

to get lost. Critic Rupert Christiansen recalled queuing
overnight to get tickets to hear Freni and Domingo in the
production, only to feel disappointed because 'this isn't an
opera which takes kindly to big stars and flash sets'.[10] James
Oestreich of *The New York Times* encapsulates here some
of the paradoxes and pragmatic considerations of this production: 'The single donkey and the single horse crossing
the stage [in Act 2] always seem gratuitous, and you have to
wonder how long such conspicuous consumption can survive amid the company's current budgetary constraints. Yet
the spectacle invariably elicits applause, and the production
is one of the few that still guarantee crowds'.[11]

The Met has recently retired a number of classic productions, but general manager Peter Gelb has, at least
at the time of writing, resisted the temptation to replace
Zeffirelli's *Bohème*. Critic Zachary Woolfe accounts for
the fact that this production 'remains untouchable' on the

grounds that 'We seem to have an almost instinctive desire for this piece to remain the same, to be the opera we encountered as children'.[12] Nostalgia evidently runs deeply through this opera, not only in its subject matter but also in the way in which it is often performed and received. Although it is hard to accept the idea that all or even a majority of audience members saw *La bohème* in childhood, there is evidently some plausibility in the idea that many look forward to it coming around again and again with comforting familiarity and in the same trappings. There is a rather ritualistic quality to the performance of *La bohème* in certain contexts and it may be that the opera's Christmas setting contributes to it, just as ballet audiences relish watching the same version of *The Nutcracker* as part of their annual festive routine.

Copley's London production, meanwhile, was recently put to bed after forty-one years, twenty-six revivals, and well over two hundred performances, and like Zeffirelli's its cast lists served as a roster of all the biggest names in opera of the last half century.[13] (Katia Ricciarelli and Plácido Domingo were the production's first Mimì and Rodolfo, and subsequent interpreters included Carreras, Pavarotti, Cotrubaş, Te Kanawa, Gheorghiu, and more.) Julia Trevelyan Oman's designs for Copley played exuberantly into the opera's invitation to visual excess, with a vast number of props. The designs were also noteworthy for their scrupulous attention to period detail: Oman went so far as to research the painter François Léopold Tabar, believed to have inspired the role of Murger's Marcel, and to commission a copy of one of Tabar's paintings. Spectacle was the order of the day: the designer created a lavish three-storey Café Momus, including a mezzanine-level billiard room that reminded Copley of one he had seen on a visit to a Left Bank café in his student days. Even this, however, was only included in the production after Oman had found an appropriate historical reference to justify it.[14]

Copley's production had, itself, replaced another long-running staging at Covent Garden: astonishingly, one that had been on the go since 1899.[15] This created a curious sense of a symbolic legacy: step just one production back and you could touch something of the composer's own time. The final run of Copley's production in summer 2015 was accompanied by celebratory events and a special publicity campaign that included flyers inviting audience members to 'Fall in love, one last time'. This sense of an ending was accompanied by a pronounced degree of nervous speculation from critics about the production by Richard Jones that was to replace it in 2017.

When Jones's *La bohème* was eventually staged, it turned out not to be the radical updating that many had feared. The production, with sets by Stewart Laing, offered imaginative touches within an ostensibly conventional staging. Particularly striking was the way in which Jones and Laing eschewed the usual pavement café in Act 2 in favour of a highly attractive recreation of the Parisian arcades— evoking the preferred environs of the quintessential Baudelairean *flâneur*—which then moved aside to reveal the interior of the Café Momus. This production also fixed the problem of the usual implausibly vast garret by creating the skeleton of a plywood attic well within the proscenium arch, seen by the audience in cut-away. Ultimately, however, the Royal Opera opted for a relatively conservative period production that seemed to have been conceived with longevity in mind.

MODERNISING STRATEGIES

Nineteenth-century-style productions live on in *Bohème*-world, then. Some are beautiful, moving, and enduringly effective. (A personal favourite is the production directed by Giancarlo del Monaco for the Teatro Real Madrid, sensitively acted by Inva Mula and Aquiles Machado in a performance available on DVD from Opus Arte.) Others now appear stale, quaint, and even kitsch. The floppy hats, checked trousers, and cravats worn by Puccini's original Bohemians and countless subsequent interpreters of the roles can seem faintly ridiculous to present-day eyes.

But *La bohème* is also eminently updateable: its slimness of plot and the enduring cultural trope of Bohemian life—still resonant and so easy to imbue with a 'hipster' twist—mean that the opera lends itself easily to being transplanted to other periods. The privations of student life, the joys and sorrows of first love, play equally convincingly if relocated to the 1930s, the 1960s, or the present. Something has to be done about the precise nature of Mimì's illness—cancer is now usually indicated as the cause, though we must surely anticipate numerous Covid-19 productions—but otherwise, little suspension of disbelief is required. Here, incidentally, *La bohème* stands up better to updating than what we might call its 'companion opera', *La traviata*, wherein the threat to the respectability of Alfredo's unseen sister certainly poses a problem of plausibility in a present-day context.

Puccini was incredibly specific about how he wanted his opera to look, the props that should be used, and even how the singers should move around the stage. Consider, for example, the following meticulous description that heads the score: 'IN THE ATTIC. Spacious window from which one sees an expanse of snow-clad roofs, on left a fireplace. A table, a small cupboard, a little book-case, four chairs, a picture easel, a bed; a few books, many packs of cards, two candlesticks. Door in the middle; another on left'.[16] This particular instruction could just as well describe a present-day apartment as a garret from the 1830s, which is one of the reasons why the opera is so easy to update, although few directors nowadays will feel the obligation to follow Puccini's instructions to the letter.

However, the sheer amount of visual clutter that Puccini's notes call for makes this an opera that does not really lend itself well to abstraction. Some of the opera's objects—the stove, the bonnet, Mimì's handwarmer—are essential to its plotline, integral to the work's focus on a certain type of disorderly domesticity, and even invested with emotional symbolism. Others may be more dispensable. There have, nevertheless, been very few minimalist productions of this work, in contrast to Wagner's music dramas, which—in a tradition dating back to the innovative early-twentieth-century productions by Adolphe Appia—have often been performed against stark white or black backdrops with few pieces of stage furniture or props. One of the most pared-down productions of *Bohème* was Robert Carsen's for Opera Vlaanderen in 1993, in which the 'garret' is merely a small diamond in the middle of the stage (containing desk, easel, and stove), surrounded by sheets of paper in Act 1 and a sea of yellow flowers to symbolise the arrival of spring in Act 4, the backdrop completely blank.

La bohème has also largely escaped the excesses of *Regietheater*. This is to some extent on account of the limitations of the opera's subject matter. It is not a work that deals with complex issues of power, politics, or corruption, or with individuals who are placed in difficult moral quandaries. The opera's gentle narrative has not endeared it to directors who favour gratuitous nudity or violence. That said, some have played up the opera's edgier qualities, or tinkered with the characterisation to make the plot more contemporary. Phyllida Lloyd's much-revived 1993 staging for Opera North—relocated to the 1960s—turned Schaunard into a drag queen and Colline into his partner. This production was a resolutely unromantic treatment of urban poverty: as Tim Ashley remarked in *The Guardian*, 'You can almost smell the damp in the concrete walls of the studio'.[17] David McVicar's 2000 production for Glyndebourne, meanwhile, set in turn-of-the-millennium squalor, came up with some ingenious fixes for dramatic details that no longer worked in the updated setting. As Andrew Clements summarises:

> In the first act Rodolfo fuses the lights in the flat to produce the darkness that has Mimi trying to light a candle, while the Cafe Momus becomes a glitzy bar, complete with flouncing waiters, silly Christmas hats, street performers and a throng of Christmas shoppers. In the third act the city gates of the original become the shuttered entrance to a tube station, and Marcello is painting a mural for the seedy club next door, while the Bohemians, back together in their flat for the final scene, snort cocaine (except for Rodolfo) just before the dying Mimi appears.[18]

Drug taking, indeed, has become something of a standard dramatic device in updated stagings of the opera. A notorious production by Ken Russell from the 1984 Macerata Festival led the way in having Mimì die of a drug overdose—earning the threat of a lawsuit from Puccini's grandson.[19] By the time Benedict Andrews used a similar conceit in 2015 for English National Opera (a co-production with Dutch National Opera)—his Rodolfo inviting his Mimì to shoot up within minutes of their meeting—such gestures appeared relatively tame by the standards of contemporary *Regietheater*. They still had the capacity to aggravate, but perhaps more because of over-familiarity than moral outrage. Rupert Christiansen of *The Telegraph* wrote that the production's concept was 'yawningly old hat', noting that he had recently seen no fewer than five others along similar lines.[20]

But this production's worst sin, this critic argued, was its failure to engage (or at least to engage him, for he reported an enthusiastic audience response). This was in part the fault of an unspecified modern setting that, according to Christiansen, 'drains all the emotional warmth from the plot and adds nothing illuminating in compensation'. And, in part, it was the fault of the lovers falling in love in a drug-fuelled haze, leading this reviewer to quip 'how is that for old-fashioned romance?' This, then, is a part of the problem: what price a *Bohème* that does not pull at the heartstrings? Mark Berry has gone so far the other way as to argue that 'In this of all operas, there is surely an imperative, albeit incessantly flouted, to rid a staging of every last ounce of sentimentality'.[21] But is the sentimentality that audiences either love or loathe in Puccini's work—unquestionably a defining feature of the work at its time of conception—at odds with more contemporary, radical methods of staging?

NEW VISIONS

Certainly, *La bohème* has rarely been drastically reinvented by avant-garde directors. It is not a work that seems to have appealed, for example, to Calixto Bieito or Peter Sellars. We might go so far as to contend that the opera resists being given a 'concept': works by Wagner or Mozart arguably lend themselves better to being treated as a blank canvas than do the works of Puccini or Strauss, where the look of the piece tends to be written into the work itself to a greater extent. There have, however, been a couple of significant attempts to challenge this assumption, including the aforementioned surreal 'lunar' *Bohème* by Claus Guth for Paris, staged as a hallucination on a defective spacecraft. Before the production opened, Guth promised that 'The second the curtain opens, you have a fist in your face'.[22] Unfortunately for Guth, some reviewers were inclined to punch back. Suzanne Lay-Canessa on the website Bachtrack, for instance, described the staging as 'saugrenu' (preposterous), while Shirley Apthorpe of *The Financial Times* remarked: 'Quite what this has to do with Puccini's *La bohème* is anybody's guess'.[23]

Another ground-breaking production was Stefan Herheim's radically interventionist 2012 *La bohème* for the Norwegian National Opera, available on DVD, which deserves detailed consideration.[24] The production goes further than any of which I am aware in fundamentally reworking the opera's narrative, even while leaving the libretto intact. Hard-hitting from the start, it opens with Mimì dying of cancer in a hospital ward before the opera commences (see figure 5.2), with the action-proper playing out as a sort of flashback in Rodolfo's imagination. However, this production's temporal setting is made deliberately ambiguous: the action switches back and forth between the present-day hospital and a conventional, nineteenth-century setting. (In a reflexive gesture probably only spotted by local opera regulars, the sections in period dress use and recontextualise sets and costumes from the previous Oslo production, first staged in 1963.) Furthermore, the two settings often merge: the hospital bed and medical equipment remain present on the stage

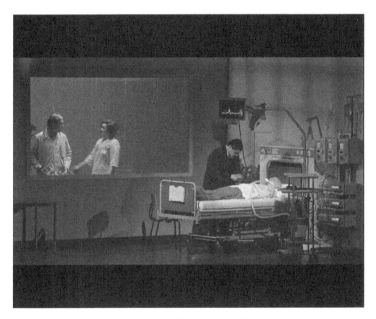

FIGURE 5.2 *La bohème*, dir. Stefan Herheim, The Norwegian National Opera, Oslo, 2012. Still from Nordic Stories / Electric Picture DVD under Fair Use rules.

during the scenes in the garret. Whether Herheim is making a point about the constructed nature of historical representations or simply saying 'people in the past were just like us' is open to speculation.

One of the British critics who reviewed the first performance of *La bohème* in Turin in 1896 welcomed 'the poignant but not over-harrowing naturalness of the sad ending'.[25] By contrast, Herheim's vision of death—cold, sterile, lonely— is unquestionably harrowing, and he presses the point that it will come to us all by employing a sinister grim reaper figure who pops up again and again as the bit-part characters Benoît, Alcindoro, and Parpignol. Even the jolly patrons of the Café Momus and the cheerful children of Act 2 are revealed to be suffering from cancer when they remove what turn out to be wigs. Anecdote suggests that some viewers found the production deeply distressing: for the sake of the recently bereft in the audience one wonders whether it might even be a production that requires some sort of 'trigger warning'.

Herheim's production has been critically acclaimed. A dissenter might argue, however, that this director goes too far in distorting the subtleties of the opera's carefully planned dramatic structure, as the contrasts of levity and profundity that are so fundamental to Puccini's dramaturgy in the opera are jeopardised, or even completely lost. Death hangs over the proceedings so relentlessly that most of the humour no longer seems humorous. The impact of the reprise in Act 4 of the love music from Act 1 is also arguably diminished because we feel little nostalgia for earlier 'happy' times, which were themselves already tinged with tragedy in this production. The end of the opera has the potential to seem less powerful, in other words, when shade has no accompanying light.

On the other hand, Herheim certainly succeeds in reinforcing what the opera is *really* about: a very young woman dying in poverty. As we laugh at the Bohemians' jolly japes and enjoy our interval drinks at the average pretty performance of *La bohème*, the harsh realities of its subject matter are often easy to overlook. Some audience members will love Herheim's radical reinterpretation, others will loathe it, but it undoubtedly prompts us to think more deeply about Puccini's opera and the way in which it confronts life's big questions.

In spite of these genuinely new takes on *La bohème*, *New York Times* critic Zachary Woolfe has recently asked whether there is only so much one can really do with Puccini's opera. Pondering if it is essentially a case of moving the stove from stage right to left to centre, he argues: 'When a director sets Wagner's "Ring" cycle at, say, the dawn of industrialisation, it illuminates new aspects of a deep, ambiguous work. But while doing "Bohème" in the 1950s or, à la "Rent," in the AIDS-era East Village may involve a change of clothes, it's still the same, simple love story'.[26] One can see something of Woolfe's point, but such a view seems more than a little unfair on Puccini, a twist on the old stereotype that he was a composer who 'knew his limitations' and was capable of working only within a restricted emotional and dramatic orbit.

The cultural meanings of operas—just like those of novels, plays, or paintings—usually do not remain static.

Rather they may take on new resonances as their themes interact with the topical events or social preoccupations of a given historical moment. An opera such as the widely pilloried *Tosca*, for example, famously dismissed by the American musicologist Joseph Kerman in 1956 as a 'shabby little shocker', suddenly seems to take on a new urgency and relevance at a moment when exploitative sexual relationships by powerful men in the public eye have come under the spotlight.[27] *La bohème*'s meanings, too, have changed over time and will do so again. (Indeed, the contemporary relevance of the piece at the time of writing, amid the Covid-19 crisis, seems pronounced.) Thus, productions such as Herheim's—which juxtaposes cosy familiarity with the jolt of a hard-hitting documentary—show that there is potential to rethink the ways in which the opera is presented in genuinely creative ways, while leaving plenty of space in the market for more conventional, crowd-pleasing productions.

It is perhaps time to reappraise not only the ways in which we perform *La bohème* but also our view of the opera itself, more or less a century on from Puccini's death. Music histories have typically dismissed Puccini's works as remnants of a dying nineteenth-century tradition, even those written in or close to the 1920s. But as we move further into the twenty-first century, we surely have sufficient distance and perspective to realise that *La bohème* was in many respects a work ahead of its time—in the ways in which it uses music to create drama, in its imaginative blend of romance and realism, even in its self-aware treatment of the subject of fantasy and make-believe. Indeed, *La bohème* prompts us to think about how we might define the 'modern' in music in fresh ways, not only in terms of harmonic language but in terms of the ways in which a work interacts with the preoccupations of its time and continues to speak meaningfully to later generations of audiences. Similarly, it makes for a particularly interesting case study as we reappraise whether theatrical works that blurred the boundaries between the serious and the popular, or that were in some sense 'international', were in fact as problematic as they have been viewed historically.

Puccini created, in *La bohème*, an opera that is simultaneously thought-provoking and enjoyable, that can hold its head high within its own sphere at the same time as having been extremely successful in entering the wider public consciousness. These things seem worth celebrating, and in our postmodern times, we can surely—finally—put to bed the anxiety that an artwork might be contaminated by contact with the recording or film industry, or with celebrity culture. *La bohème* is far more than a mere warhorse; rather, it continues to have immensely important cultural currency. It has become, quite simply, one of those tales that needs to be told and retold.

NOTES

INTRODUCTION

1 For wider reading, see: Arthur Groos and Roger Parker, eds., *Giacomo Puccini: La bohème* (Cambridge: Cambridge University Press, 1986); Michele Girardi, *Puccini: His International Art*, trans. Laura Basini (Chicago and London: University of Chicago Press, 2000); and Julian Budden, *Puccini: His Life and Works* (Oxford: Oxford University Press, 2002).

2 Herbert Lindenberger, *Situating Opera: Period, Genre, Reception* (Cambridge: Cambridge University Press, 2010), 39.

3 Anon., 'Production of Puccini's *La bohème* at the Metropolitan', *The New York Times*, 30 December 1900, 20.

4 Alexandra Wilson, *The Puccini Problem: Opera, Nationalism, and Modernity* (Cambridge: Cambridge University Press, 2007).

5 Vincent Seligman, *Puccini among Friends* (London: MacMillan, 1938), 31.

CHAPTER 1

1 For a comparison of the two operas, see Allan W. Atlas, 'Mimì's Death: Mourning in Puccini and Leoncavallo', *Journal of Musicology* 14, no. 1 (Winter 1996): 52–79.

2 Cited in Budden, *Puccini: His Life and Works*, 143.

3 Anon., 'The Bohemians', *Liverpool Mercury*, 23 April 1897, 5.

4 Henry Edward Krehbiel, *Chapters of Opera, Being Historical and Critical Observations and Records Concerning the Lyric Drama in New York from its Earliest Days Down to the Present Time* (New York: Da Capo Press, 1980), 286. This text is a reprint of the revised 2nd edn. (New York: H. Holt, 1909).

5 W. J. Henderson, 'Puccini's *La bohème*', *New York Times*, 27 December 1900, 6.

6 Anon., 'Puccini's *La bohème* Sung in Italian Last Night at Wallack's Theatre', *New York Times*, 17 May 1898, 6.

7 For further reading, see Andrew Davis, *Il Trittico, Turandot, and Puccini's Late Style* (Bloomington: Indiana University Press, 2010).

8 Arman Schwartz, 'Realism and Skepticism in Puccini's Early Operas', in *Giacomo Puccini and his World*, ed. Arman Schwartz and Emanuele Senici (Princeton: Princeton University Press, 2016), 29–48, 41–44.

9 'The Homer of Seville', *The Simpsons*, Season 19, Episode 2, Fox Network, 2007.

10 Cited in Budden, *Puccini: His Life and Works*, 140.

11 Luc Sante, *The Other Paris* (London: Faber and Faber, 2015), 153.

12 Reproduced in Nicholas John, ed., *La bohème* (London: John Calder, 1982), 49.

13 The libretto for this missing act is reproduced in Groos and Parker, eds., *Giacomo Puccini: La bohème*, 142–81.

14 '. . . sa mort est une des choses les plus émouvantes et les mieux présentées que nous ayons vues au théâtre depuis longtemps'. Albert Montel, 'Chronique musicale', *Le XIX siècle*, 15 June 1898, n.p.; Anon., 'Puccini's *La bohème* at Manchester', *London Daily News*, 24 April 1897, 6.

15 Lindenberger, *Situating Opera*, 137.

16 For a fuller analysis of Mimì's death scene, see Helen Greenwald, 'Ars moriendi: Reflections on the Death of Mimì', in *The Arts of the Prima Donna in the Long 19th Century*, ed. Rachel Cowgill and Hilary Poriss (New York: Oxford University Press, 2012), 167–85.

17 Cited in Budden, *Puccini: His Life and Works*, 136.

18 Kunio Hara, 'Staging Nostalgia in Puccini's Operas' (Ph.D. diss., Indiana University, 2012), 6.

19 Stephen Williams, *Come to the Opera!* (London: Hutchinson and Co., 1948), 131.

20 Hara, 'Staging Nostalgia in Puccini's Operas', 20.

CHAPTER 2

1 Cited in Walter L. Adamson, *Avant-Garde Florence: From Modernism to Fascism* (Cambridge, MA and London: Harvard University Press, 1993), 25.

2 Such artists included Giovanni Boldini, Giuseppe De Nittis, and Telemaco Signorini. Roberta J. M. Olson, ed., *Ottocento: Romanticism and Revolution in 19th-Century Italian Painting* (New York: The American Federation of Arts, 1992), 31.

3 Claudio Sartori, *Puccini* (Milan: Nuova Accademia Editrice, 1958), 155–56.

4 See, for example, ibid., 157.

5 Dante Del Fiorentino, *Immortal Bohemian: An Intimate Memoir of Giacomo Puccini* (London: Victor Gollancz, 1952).

6 Girardi, *Puccini: His International Art*, 114–15.

7 Ibid., 115.

8 Olga Haldey, ' "La bohème" à la Russe and the Puccini Politics of Late Nineteenth-Century Russia', *Opera Journal* 37, no. 4 (December 2004): 3–19, 5.

9 Thomas Burke, *Nights in Town: A London Autobiography* (London: George Allen and Unwin, 1915).

10 Anon., 'London Theatres: The Royal Covent Garden', *The Stage*, 6 July 1899, 13.

11 G. Salvayre, 'Premières représentations', *Gil Blas*, 14 June 1898, n.p.

12 Charles-A. Garnier, 'Les Premières', *La Justice*, 16 June 1898, 1.

13 Alfred Bruneau, 'Les Théâtres', *Le Figaro*, 14 June 1898, 4.

14 Richard Specht, *Giacomo Puccini: The Man, His Life, His Work*, trans. Catherine Alison Phillips (London and Toronto: J. M. Dent and Sons, 1933), 2.

15 Joanna Richardson, *The Bohemians: La Vie de Bohème in Paris 1830–1914* (London: MacMillan, 1969), 11.

16 Seligman, *Puccini among Friends*, 31.

17 Jonathan Rose, *The Intellectual Life of the British Working Classes*, 2nd edn. (New Haven and London: Yale University Press, 2010), 447.

18 Jerrold Seigel, 'The Rise of Bohemia', in *Giacomo Puccini: La bohème*, ed. Groos and Parker, 1–11, 1.

19 Anon., 'Carl Rosa Company', *The Era*, 9 October 1897, 9.

20 Charles Rearick, *Paris Dreams, Paris Memories: The City and Its Mystique* (Stanford: Stanford University Press, 2011), 37.

21 For further reading on Parisian street music, and particularly the decline of street hawkers—so central to the soundworld of Old Paris—as the city was regenerated, see Jacek Blaszkiewicz, 'City Myths: Music and Urbanism in Second-Empire Paris' (Ph.D. diss., University of Rochester, 2018).

22 'Je ne crois pas avoir besoin de vous présenter les principaux personnages de *La Vie de Bohème*; vous les connaissez'. E. Reyer, 'Revue musicale', *Journal des débats*, 26 June 1898, 1–2, 1.

23 Rearick, *Paris Dreams*, 34.

24 Michela Ronzani, 'Creating Success and Forming Imaginaries: The Innovative Publicity Campaign for Puccini's La bohème', in *The Idea of Art Music in a Commercial World, 1800–1930*, ed. Christina Bashford and Roberta Montemorra Marvin (Woodbridge: The Boydell Press, 2016), 39–59, 56.

25 See Rearick, *Paris Dreams*, 7–9.

26 Ibid., 30–31.

27 Ibid., 29–30.

28 Anon., 'The Bohemians', *Musical Times* 38, no. 652 (1 June 1897): 402.

29 Groos and Parker, *Giacomo Puccini: La bohème*, 13.

30 See Fourcaud, 'Musique', *Le Gaulois*, 14 June 1898, n.p., and Fernande Le Borne, 'La Vie de Bohème', *Le Monde artiste*, 19 June 1898, 389–90, 389.

31 David Kimbell argues that 'What the opera conspicuously does not do is to reinforce Murger's moral warnings about the danger of lingering too long in Bohemia . . . Still less does it attempt to make his story a document in the cause of Socialist realism as the Italian translator Camerone urged'. David Kimbell, *Italian Opera* (Cambridge: Cambridge University Press, 1991), 588.

32 As Julian Budden puts it: 'Far from being underprivileged, [Murger's] Bohemians are young men of the middle class sewing their wild oats. Their language, by turns slangy and bombastic, is that of students the world over, their poverty self inflicted'. Budden, *Puccini: His Life and Works*, 136.

33 Wakeling Dry, *Giacomo Puccini* (London and New York: John Lane, 1906), 72.

34 Ibid., 73–74.

35 Philip Page, 'Realism in Opera', *London Mercury* 18, no. 105 (July 1928): 290–97, 296.

36 See, for example, E. Reyer, 'Revue musicale', *Journal des débats*, 26 June 1898, 1–2.

CHAPTER 3

1 Cited in Eugenio Gara, ed., *Carteggi Pucciniani* (Milan: Ricordi, 1958), 141n.

2 Budden, *Puccini: His Life and Works*, 156.

3 William Ashbrook, 'A Brief Stage History', in *La bohème*, ed. Groos and Parker, 115–28, 120.

4 For a full treatment of the Ricordi publicity campaign, see Ronzani, 'Creating Success and Forming Imaginaries'.

5 On Viennese responses to the opera see Sandra McColl, *Music Criticism in Vienna 1896–1897: Critically Moving Forms* (Oxford: Clarendon Press, 1996).

6 Haldey, ' "La bohème" à la Russe', 4–5.

7 Herman Klein, 'The Gramophone and the Singer', *Gramophone*, October 1929, 189–91, 189.

8 Anon., 'Our London Correspondence', *Manchester Guardian*, 3 July 1899, 7.

9 Musicus, 'Music and the Drama', *Sheffield Independent*, 2 January 1899, 7.

10 Ashbrook, 'A Brief Stage History', 123; Herman Klein, *The Golden Age of Opera* (London: George Routledge and Sons, 1933), 224.

11 Anon., 'Puccini's *La bohème* Sung in Italian Last Night at Wallack's Theatre', *New York Times*, 17 May 1898, 6.

12 Krehbiel, *Chapters of Opera*, 285.

13 Anon., 'Litigation over *La bohème*', *New York Times*, 10 October 1898, n.p.

14 All of the following data on performances at the New York Met is taken from the Metropolitan Opera archives database, unless otherwise indicated, https://www.metopera.org/discover/archives/.

15 Henderson, 'Puccini's *La bohème*', 6.

16 Seligman, *Puccini among Friends*, 37.

17 For further reading, see Wilson, *The Puccini Problem*, 40–68.

18 William Ashbrook, 'Some Aspects of *La bohème*', in *La bohème*, ed. Gary Kahn (Overture Publishing: London, 2010), 9–16, 10.

19 Fernande Le Borne, 'La Vie de Bohême', *Le Monde artiste*, 19 June 1898, 389–90, 389.

20 Arthur Pougin, 'Semaine théatrale', *Le Ménestrel*, 19 June 1898, 194–96, 194.

21 Albert Montel, 'Chronique musicale', *Le XIX siècle*, 15 June 1898, n.p.

22 'Nous aurions été fortement déçus si d'un compositeur italien ne nous était pas venue une partition italienne'. E. Reyer, 'Revue musicale', *Journal des débats*, 26 June 1898, 1–2, 2.

23 'Abandonando a rotina que vivia das ephêmeras glorias rossinianas, Puccini foi procurar na escola alemã o tônico que poderia reconstituir a musica italiana'. Anon., 'Theatros e Musica', *Jornal do Commercio*, 4 July 1897, 2.

24 Cited in McColl, *Music Criticism in Vienna*, 207, 211.

25 Henry-Louis de la Grange, *Gustav Mahler, Vol. 2 Vienna: The Years of Challenge (1897–1904)* (Oxford and New York: Oxford University Press, 1995), 23.

26 Cited in Haldey, ' "La bohème" à la Russe', 11.

27 'Veritas', '*La bohème* di Puccini', *Il Secolo*, 3–4 February 1896, n.p.

28 Henderson, 'Puccini's *La bohème*', 6.

29 McColl, *Music Criticism in Vienna*, 215, 212.

30 Haldey, ' "La bohème" à la Russe', 9.

31 'Les licences que s'est permises M. Puccini peuvent faire grincer des dents, comme quand on mord dans une pomme verte, à quelques puristes: je ne m'en inquiète pas'. E. Reyer, 'Revue musicale', *Journal des débats*, 26 June 1898, 1–2, 2.

32 F. Bonavia, 'Giacomo Puccini and Ferruccio Busoni', *Music & Letters* 6, no. 2 (April 1925): 99–109, 102.

33 Cited in Wilson, *The Puccini Problem*, 67.

34 Reported in Anon., 'Music', *The Illustrated Sporting and Dramatic News*, 9 May 1896, 351.

35 'No se registra en las representaciones de la actual compañía de ópera italiana, un triunfo más completo que el obtenido en el estreno de la obra de Puccini, la noche del sábado. El joven compositor italiano que ha recibido ovaciones en todos los principales teatros de Europa, recibió también la del público mexicano. Al principio se mostró el auditorio bastante reservado, pero ya al final del primer cuadro estaba vencido, y concedía nutridos aplausos a la obra y á los artistas'. Anon., 'La Bohemia', *La Voz de México*, 24 August 1897, 2.

36 Cited in McColl, *Music Criticism in Vienna*, 205.

37 Anon., 'Production of Puccini's *La bohème* at the Metropolitan', 20.

38 Henry Krehbiel, untitled review in *The New York Tribune*, n.d., reproduced on the Met Archive.

39 De la Grange, *Gustav Mahler*, 2:23.

40 Anon., 'The Musical World', *St James's Gazette*, 4 October 1897, 12.

41 Anon., '*La bohème* at Covent Garden', *The Pall Mall Gazette*, 4 October 1897, 3.

42 B. W. F., 'Music', *The Illustrated Sporting and Dramatic News*, 8 July 1899, 734.

43 'Ce qui caractérice [*sic*] ces quatre actes de la *Bohême* c'est de plaire en même temps aux yeux et aux oreilles. Le coeur aussi y trouve son compte et on sort de ce spectacle après avoir ri et un peu pleuré. Que voulez-vous de plus?' Albert Montel, 'Chronique musicale', *Le XIX siècle*, 15 June 1898, n.p.

44 Arthur Pougin, 'Semaine théatrale', *Le Ménestrel*, 19 June 1898, 194–96, 196.

45 Ibid., 195.

46 E. N., 'Soirée Parisienne', *Le Gaulois*, 14 June 1898, n.p.

47 G. Salvayre, 'Premières représentations', *Gil Blas*, 14 June 1898, n.p. See also Fernande Le Borne, 'La Vie de Bohême', *Le Monde artiste*, 19 June 1898, 389–90, 389.

48 See, for example, Alfred Bruneau, 'Les Théâtres', *Le Figaro*, 14 June 1898, 4.

49 Anon., 'The Musical World', *St James's Gazette*, 4 October 1897, 12.

50 Anon., 'The Bohemians', *Liverpool Mercury*, 23 April 1897, 5. Frederick Clive Newcome (1847–94) was best known for his depictions of mountain scenes.

51 For example Anon., 'The History of *La Vie de Bohème*', *The Era*, 2 October 1897, 13, and Our Own Correspondent, 'Puccini's "The Bohemians"', *The Scotsman*, 23 April 1897, 5.

52 Kimberly J. Stern, 'Rule Bohemia: The Cosmopolitics of Subculture in George du Maurier's *Trilby*', *Victorian Literature and Culture* 38, no. 2 (2010): 547–70, 547.

53 Cited in Harry Stopes, 'Provincial Modernity: Manchester and Lille in Transnational Perspective, 1860–1914' (Ph.D. diss., University College London, 2017), 140. Joanna Richardson writes 'Nineteenth-century England produced its eccentrics, its aesthetes and its socially unorthodox writers and artists, but there was no sense of a Bohemian movement'. Joanna Richardson, 'Henry Murger and "la vie de bohème"', in *La bohème*, ed. Kahn, 41–50, 41.

54 Anon., 'Plançon sings "Marseillaise"', *New York Times*, undated review, Metropolitan Opera archive database.

55 Ashbrook, 'A Brief Stage History', 121–22.

56 Dry, *Giacomo Puccini*, 68.

57 Seligman, *Puccini among Friends*, 35.

58 Ibid., 36.

59 Ibid., 40.

60 'C'è l'opera di teatro, e non la tesi di laurea'. Adriano Lualdi, *Serate musicali* (Milan: Fratelli Treves Editori, 1928), 51.

CHAPTER 4

1 D. C. Parker, 'A View of Giacomo Puccini', *Musical Quarterly* 3, no. 4 (October 1917): 509–16, 509.

2 See Wilson, *The Puccini Problem*.

3 Parker, 'A View of Giacomo Puccini', 509.

4 Thomas Beecham, *A Mingled Chime: Leaves from an Autobiography* (London: Hutchison & Co., 1948), 50.

5 See, for example, Specht, *Giacomo Puccini*, ix.

6 Parker, 'A View of Giacomo Puccini', 514–15.

7 G. Jean-Aubry, 'The New Italy', *Musical Quarterly* 6, no. 1 (January 1920): 29–56, 29.

8 Fausto Torrefranca, *Giacomo Puccini e l'opera internazionale* (Turin: Bocca, 1912). See also Alexandra Wilson, 'Torrefranca vs. Puccini: Embodying a Decadent Italy', *Cambridge Opera Journal* 13, no. 1 (2001): 29–53.

9 Torrefranca, *Giacomo Puccini*, 30, 76, 78.

10 Jean-Aubry, 'The New Italy', 36.

11 Ibid., 55.

12 Compton Mackenzie, *My Record of Music* (London: Hutchinson, 1955), 56.

13 Dry, *Giacomo Puccini*, 73.

14 Haldey, ' "La bohème" à la Russe', 6.

15 Nellie Melba, *Melodies and Memories* (London: Thornton Butterworth, 1925), 115.

16 Anon., 'Production of Puccini's *La bohème* at the Metropolitan', 20.

17 Anon., 'Royal Opera, Covent Garden', *The Era*, 26 May 1900, 8.

18 R. A. N., 'Musical News', *County Gentleman: Sporting Gazette, Agricultural Journal*, 26 May 1900, 649.

19 Ernest Newman, 'Acting in Opera I: Some Special Difficulties', *Sunday Times*, 16 June 1935, cited in Ernest Newman, *From the World of Music* (London: John Calder, 1956), 46–49, 47–48.

20 J. B. Steane, *Singers of the Century: Volume 2* (London: Duckworth, 1998), 148.

21 For a complete list of all the *La bohème* recordings to 2012, see Roger Flury, *Giacomo Puccini: A Discography* (Lanham, Toronto and Plymouth: The Scarecrow Press, 2012), 91–286.

22 G. M. Thomson, 'Britain's Favourite Gramophone Records', *Strand Magazine*, January 1929, 70–77, 72.

23 Compton Mackenzie, 'Editorial', *Gramophone*, May 1928, 483–86, 486.

24 James Caskett, 'Review of Records', *Gramophone*, August 1923, 59–60, 60.

25 Anon., 'Translations', *Gramophone*, April 1924, 224–25, 225.

26 For further reading, see Julie Brown, 'Framing the Atmospheric Film Prologue in Britain, 1919–1926', in *The Sounds of the Silents in Britain*, ed. Julie Brown and Annette Davison (New York: Oxford University Press, 2013), 200–221.

27 Ken Wlaschin, *Encyclopedia of Opera on Screen: A Guide to More than 100 Years of Opera Films, Videos and DVDs* (New Haven and London: Yale University Press, 2004), 82.

28 Ibid., 84.

29 Anon., 'Turning Opera into Fox-Trots', *Musical Mirror* 3, no. 11 (November 1923): 329.

30 Specht, *Giacomo Puccini*, 4.

31 Marcia J. Citron discusses the film's use of opera in detail in '"An Honest Contrivance": Opera and Desire in *Moonstruck*', *Music & Letters* 89, no. 1 (February 2008): 56–83.

32 For further reading see Alexandra Wilson, 'Unreliable Authors, Unreliable History: Opera in Joe Wright's Adaptation of *Atonement*', *Cambridge Opera Journal* 27, no. 2 (2015): 155–74.

33 'Passion', *Buffy the Vampire Slayer*, Season 2, episode 17, WB Television Network, 1998.

34 Caryl Flinn, 'Embracing Kitsch: Werner Schroeter, Music, and The Bomber Pilot', in *Film Music: Critical Approaches*, ed. Kevin J. Donnelly (Edinburgh: Edinburgh University Press, 2001), 129–51, 130.

35 A less than enthusiastic review can be found here: David Rooney, '"Breathe Umphefumlo": Berlin Review', *The Hollywood Reporter*, 2 August 2015, accessed 12 November 2019, https://www.hollywoodreporter.com/review/breathe-umphefumlo-berlin-review-771070.

36 Rupert Christiansen, '*La Bohème*, Isango Ensemble, Hackney Empire, review', *The Telegraph*, 23 May 2012, accessed 13 November 2019, https://www.telegraph.co.uk/culture/music/opera/9284988/La-Boheme-Isango-Ensemble-Hackney-Empire-review.html.

37 Anthony Tommasini, 'Like Opera Inspiring It, *Rent* Is Set to Endure', *New York Times*, 5 September 2008, accessed 12 November 2019, https://www.nytimes.com/2008/09/06/arts/music/06rent.html.

38 Mina Yang, '*Moulin Rouge!* And the Undoing of Opera', *Cambridge Opera Journal* 20, no. 3 (November 2008): 269–82, 271.

39 Parker, 'A View of Giacomo Puccini', 514.

CHAPTER 5

1 Kate Molleson, 'Noseda brings a *Bohème* for our Times from Turin', *The Herald*, 16 August 2017, accessed 28 October 2018, https://www.heraldscotland.com/news/15475190.a-tragedy-in-the-way-puccini-wanted-it-to-be-told/.

2 For further reading, see Ulrich Müller, '*Regietheater*/Director's Theater', in *The Oxford Handbook of Opera*, ed. Helen Greenwald (New York: Oxford University Press, 2014), 582–605.

3 The question of operatic updating is discussed further in Tom Sutcliffe, *Believing in Opera* (London: Faber, 1996) and David J. Levin, *Unsettling Opera: Staging Mozart, Verdi, Wagner, and Zemlinsky* (Chicago: University of Chicago Press, 2007).

4 See Alexandra Wilson, 'Golden-Age Thinking: Recent Productions of *Gianni Schicchi* and the Popular Historical Imagination', *Cambridge Opera Journal* 25, no. 2 (2013): 185–201.

5 Andrew Clements, '*La bohème*, Theatre Royal Glasgow', *The Guardian*, 30 April 2004, accessed 14 June 2017, https://www.theguardian.com/music/2004/apr/30/classicalmusicandopera.

6 See, for example, https://www.theguardian.com/music/2016/jun/13/opera-holland-park-la-boheme-puccini-review, accessed 31 May 2017.

7 Mark Berry, '*La bohème*. Opera Holland Park', *Opera Today*, 16 June 2016, accessed 5 October 2017, http://www.operatoday.com/content/2016/06/la_bohme_opera_.php.

8 Ibid.

9 Jonathan Sutherland, '*La bohème* a Chilly Disappointment in Vienna', Bachtrack.com, 28 March 2016, accessed 11 July 2018, https://bachtrack.com/review-boheme-blue-borras-wiener-staatsoper-march-2016.

10 Rupert Christiansen, '*La Bohème*, Opera North, Grand Theatre, Leeds, Review', *The Telegraph*, 3 May 2014, accessed 13 November 2019, https://www.telegraph.co.uk/culture/music/opera/10806114/La-Boheme-Opera-North-Grand-Theatre-Leeds-review-hits-hard.html.

11 James R. Oestreich, 'Review: *La bohème* at the Met is Grand, Reviled and Beloved', *New York Times*, 3 October 2017, accessed 5 October 2017, https://www.nytimes.com/2017/10/03/arts/music/la-boheme-review-zeffirelli-met-opera.html.

12 Zachary Woolfe, '"La bohème": Should Opera's Most Beloved Classic be Changed?', *New York Times*, 27 October 2017, accessed 10 July 2018, https://www.nytimes.com/2017/10/27/arts/music/la-boheme-puccini-opera-metropolitan-london-paris.html.

13 Rupert Christiansen, '*La bohème*, Royal Opera House, Review', *The Telegraph*, 24 May 2015, accessed 13 November 2019, https://www.telegraph.co.uk/culture/music/opera/11624017/La-Boheme-Royal-Opera-House-review-Netrebko-Calleja.html.

14 Sarah Lenton, 'The Creation of a Classic', *La bohème* programme book, Royal Opera House, 2014–15 season, 11–17, 12, 13.

15 Ibid., 11.

16 Giacomo Puccini, *La bohème: Ricordi Opera Vocal Score Series* (Milan: Casa Ricordi Editore, 1997), 3.

17 Tim Ashley, '*La bohème*', *The Guardian*, 18 January 2010, accessed 14 June 2017, https://www.theguardian.com/music/2010/jan/18/la-boheme-phyllida-lloyd-review.

18 Andrew Clements, 'A Fresh-Faced Puccini', *The Guardian*, 12 October 2000, accessed 14 June 2017, https://www.theguardian.com/culture/2000/oct/12/artsfeatures5.

19 Alex Needham, '*La bohème* Review', *The Guardian*, 6 January 2014, accessed 14 June 2017, https://www.theguardian.com/culture/australia-culture-blog/2014/jan/06/la-boheme-review.

20 Rupert Christiansen, '*La bohème*, English National Opera, Review', *The Telegraph*, October 17 2015, accessed 14 June 2017, http://www.telegraph.co.uk/opera/what-to-see/la-boheme-english-national-opera-review/.

21 Mark Berry, '*La bohème* at the Salzburg Festival', *Opera Today*, 28 August 2012, accessed 14 June 2017, http://www.operatoday.com/content/2012/08/la_boheme_at_th.php.

22 Cited in Woolfe, '"La bohème": Should Opera's Most Beloved Classic be Changed?'.

23 Shirley Apthorp, 'A Storm of Boos for La bohème at the Paris Opera', *The Financial Times*, 4 December 2017, accessed 10 July 2018, https://www.ft.com/content/96f740fc-d8e0-11e7-9504-59efdb70e12f.

24 The journal *Opera Quarterly* considered it so significant that it commissioned a portfolio of extended responses to it. Arman Schwartz, Mark Schachtsiek, Roger Parker, Flora Willson, Alexandra Wilson, 'Stefan Herheim's *La bohème* on DVD: A Review Portfolio', *Opera Quarterly* 29, no. 2 (Spring 2013): 146–74.

25 Our Own Special Correspondent, 'Giacomo Puccini's *La bohème*', *The Pall Mall Gazette*, 12 March 1896, 2.

26 Woolfe, '"La bohème": Should Opera's Most Beloved Classic be Changed?'

27 Joseph Kerman, *Opera as Drama*, new and revised edn. (London: Faber and Faber, 1989), 206.

BIBLIOGRAPHY

NEWSPAPERS, PERIODICALS, AND REVIEW WEBSITES

Bachtrack.com
The County Gentleman: Sporting Gazette, Agricultural Journal
The Era
Le Figaro
The Financial Times
Le Gaulois
Gil Blas
Gramophone
The Guardian
The Herald
The Illustrated Sporting and Dramatic News
Jornal do Commercio
Journal des débats
La Justice
The Liverpool Mercury
The London Daily News
The London Mercury
The Manchester Guardian
Le Ménestrel
Le Monde artiste
The Musical Mirror
The Musical Times
The New York Times
The New York Tribune
Opera Today

The Pall Mall Gazette
St James's Gazette
The Scotsman
Il Secolo
Sheffield Independent
The Stage
The Strand Magazine
The Sunday Times
The Telegraph
La Voz de México
Le XIX siècle

BOOKS AND JOURNAL ARTICLES

Anon., 'The Bohemians', The Musical Times, 38/652 (1 June 1897), 402

Walter L. Adamson, Avant-Garde Florence: From Modernism to Fascism (Cambridge, MA and London: Harvard University Press, 1993)

Allan W. Atlas, 'Mimì's Death: Mourning in Puccini and Leoncavallo', Journal of Musicology, 14/1 (Winter 1996), 52–79

G. Jean-Aubry, 'The New Italy', Musical Quarterly, 6/1 (January 1920), 29–56

Thomas Beecham, A Mingled Chime: Leaves from an Autobiography (London: Hutchison & Co., 1948)

Jacek Blaszkiewicz, 'City Myths: Music and Urbanism in Second-Empire Paris', Ph.D. diss., University of Rochester, 2018

F. Bonavia, 'Giacomo Puccini and Ferruccio Busoni', Music & Letters, 6/2 (April 1925), 99–109

Julie Brown, 'Framing the Atmospheric Film Prologue in Britain, 1919–1926', in Julie Brown and Annette Davison (eds.), The Sounds of the Silents in Britain (New York: Oxford University Press, 2013), 200–221

Julian Budden, Puccini: His Life and Works (Oxford: Oxford University Press, 2002)

Thomas Burke, Nights in Town: A London Autobiography (London: George Allen and Unwin, 1915)

Marcia J. Citron, ' "An Honest Contrivance": Opera and Desire in Moonstruck', Music & Letters, 89/1 (February 2008), 56–83

Andrew Davis, Il Trittico, Turandot, and Puccini's Late Style (Bloomington: Indiana University Press, 2010)

Henry-Louis de la Grange, Gustav Mahler, vol. 2 Vienna: The Years of Challenge (1897–1904) (Oxford and New York: Oxford University Press, 1995)

Dante Del Fiorentino, Immortal Bohemian: An Intimate Memoir of Giacomo Puccini (London: Victor Gollancz Ltd., 1952)

Wakeling Dry, Giacomo Puccini (London and New York: John Lane, 1906)

Caryl Flinn, 'Embracing Kitsch: Werner Schroeter, Music, and The Bomber Pilot', in Kevin J. Donnelly (ed.), *Film Music: Critical Approaches* (Edinburgh: Edinburgh University Press, 2001), 129–51

Roger Flury, *Giacomo Puccini: A Discography* (Lanham, Toronto, and Plymouth: The Scarecrow Press, 2012)

Eugenio Gara, ed., *Carteggi Pucciniani* (Milan: Ricordi, 1958)

Michele Girardi, *Puccini: His International Art*, trans. Laura Basini (Chicago and London: University of Chicago Press, 2000)

Helen Greenwald, 'Ars moriendi: Reflections on the Death of Mimì', in Rachel Cowgill and Hilary Poriss (eds.), *The Arts of the Prima Donna in the Long 19th Century* (New York: Oxford University Press, 2012), 167–85

Arthur Groos and Roger Parker (eds.), *Giacomo Puccini: La bohème* (Cambridge: Cambridge University Press, 1986)

Olga Haldey, ' "La bohème" à la Russe and the Puccini Politics of Late Nineteenth-Century Russia', *Opera Journal*, 37/4 (December 2004), 3–19

Kunio Hara, 'Staging Nostalgia in Puccini's Operas' Ph.D. diss., Indiana University, 2012

Nicholas John (ed.), *La bohème* (London: John Calder, 1982)

Gary Kahn (ed.), *La bohème* (London: Overture Publishing, 2010)

Joseph Kerman, *Opera as Drama*, new and revised edn. (London: Faber and Faber, 1989)

David Kimbell, *Italian Opera* (Cambridge: Cambridge University Press, 1991)

Herman Klein, *The Golden Age of Opera* (London: George Routledge and Sons, 1933)

Henry Edward Krehbiel, *Chapters of Opera, Being Historical and Critical Observations and Records Concerning the Lyric Drama in New York from Its Earliest Days Down to the Present Time* (New York: Da Capo Press, 1980)

Sarah Lenton, 'The Creation of a Classic', *La bohème* programme book, *Royal Opera House*, 2014–15 season, 11–17

David J. Levin, *Unsettling Opera: Staging Mozart, Verdi, Wagner, and Zemlinsky* (Chicago: University of Chicago Press, 2007)

Herbert Lindenberger, *Situating Opera: Period, Genre, Reception* (Cambridge: Cambridge University Press, 2010)

Adriano Lualdi, *Serate musicali* (Milan: Fratelli Treves Editori, 1928)

Compton Mackenzie, *My Record of Music* (London: Hutchinson, 1955)

Sandra McColl, *Music Criticism in Vienna 1896–1897: Critically Moving Forms* (Oxford: Clarendon Press, 1996)

Nellie Melba, *Melodies and Memories* (London: Thornton Butterworth, 1925)

Ulrich Müller, 'Regietheater/Director's Theater', in Helen Greenwald (ed.), *The Oxford Handbook of Opera* (New York: Oxford University Press, 2014), 582–605

Ernest Newman, *From the World of Music* (London: John Calder, 1956)

Roberta J. M. Olson (ed.), *Ottocento: Romanticism and Revolution in 19th-Century Italian Painting* (New York: The American Federation of Arts, 1992)

D. C. Parker, 'A View of Giacomo Puccini', *Musical Quarterly*, 3/4 (October 1917), 509–16

Giacomo Puccini, *La bohème: Ricordi Opera Vocal Score Series* (Milan: Casa Ricordi Editore, 1997)

Charles Rearick, *Paris Dreams, Paris Memories: The City and Its Mystique* (Stanford: Stanford University Press, 2011)

Joanna Richardson, *The Bohemians: La Vie de Bohème in Paris 1830–1914* (London: MacMillan, 1969)

Michela Ronzani, 'Creating Success and Forming Imaginaries: The Innovative Publicity Campaign for Puccini's La bohème', in Christina Bashford and Roberta Montemorra Marvin (eds.), *The Idea of Art Music in a Commercial World, 1800–1930* (Woodbridge: The Boydell Press, 2016), 39–59

Jonathan Rose, *The Intellectual Life of the British Working Classes*, 2nd edn. (New Haven and London: Yale University Press, 2010)

Luc Sante, *The Other Paris* (London: Faber and Faber, 2015)

Claudio Sartori, *Puccini* (Milan: Nuova Accademia Editrice, 1958)

Arman Schwartz, 'Realism and Skepticism in Puccini's Early Operas', in Arman Schwartz and Emanuele Senici (eds.), *Giacomo Puccini and his World* (Princeton: Princeton University Press, 2016), 29–48

Arman Schwartz, Mark Schachtsiek, Roger Parker, Flora Willson, and Alexandra Wilson, 'Stefan Herheim's La bohème on DVD: A Review Portfolio', *Opera Quarterly*, 29/2 (Spring 2013), 146–74

Vincent Seligman, *Puccini among Friends* (London: MacMillan, 1938)

Richard Specht, *Giacomo Puccini: The Man, His Life, His Work*, trans. Catherine Alison Phillips (London and Toronto: J. M. Dent and Sons Ltd, 1933)

J. B. Steane, *Singers of the Century*, vol. 2 (London: Duckworth, 1998)

Kimberly J. Stern, 'Rule Bohemia: The Cosmopolitics of Subculture in George du Maurier's *Trilby*', *Victorian Literature and Culture*, 38/2 (2010), 547–70

Harry Stopes, 'Provincial Modernity: Manchester and Lille in Transnational Perspective, 1860–1914' Ph.D. diss., University College London, 2017

Tom Sutcliffe, *Believing in Opera* (London: Faber, 1996)

Fausto Torrefranca, *Giacomo Puccini e l'opera internazionale* (Turin: Bocca, 1912)

Stephen Williams, *Come to the Opera!* (London: Hutchinson, 1948)

Alexandra Wilson, 'Torrefranca vs. Puccini: Embodying a Decadent Italy', *Cambridge Opera Journal*, 13/1 (2001), 29–53

Alexandra Wilson, *The Puccini Problem: Opera, Nationalism, and Modernity* (Cambridge: Cambridge University Press, 2007)

Alexandra Wilson, 'Golden-Age Thinking: Recent Productions of *Gianni Schicchi* and the Popular Historical Imagination', *Cambridge Opera Journal*, 25/2 (2013), 185–201

Alexandra Wilson, 'Unreliable Authors, Unreliable History: Opera in Joe Wright's Adaptation of *Atonement*', *Cambridge Opera Journal*, 27/2 (2015), 155–74

Ken Wlaschin, *Encyclopedia of Opera on Screen: A Guide to More than 100 Years of Opera Films, Videos and DVDs* (New Haven and London: Yale University Press, 2004)

Mina Yang, '*Moulin Rouge!* And the Undoing of Opera', *Cambridge Opera Journal*, 20/3 (November 2008), 269–82

INDEX

For the benefit of digital users, indexed terms that span two pages (e.g., 52–53) may, on occasion, appear on only one of those pages.